GREAT WAR BRITAIN
MANCHESTER
Remembering 1914–18

The Sentry, 1921, commemorating employees of S&J Watts & Co.

GREAT WAR BRITAIN

MANCHESTER

Remembering 1914–18

ANDREW SIMPSON

First published 2017

The History Press
The Mill, Brimscombe Port
Stroud, Gloucestershire, GL5 2QG
www.thehistorypress.co.uk

British Library Cataloguing in Publication Data.
A catalogue record for this book is available from the British Library.

ISBN 978 0 7509 7896 5

Typesetting and origination by The History Press
Printed in Malta by Melita Press

CONTENTS

TIMELINE

1914

28 June 1914

*Assassination of Archduke
Franz Ferdinand in Sarajevo*

4 August 1914

Great Britain declares war on Germany

13 August 1914

*Internment of first batch of
German residents*

23 August 1914

Battle of Tannenberg commences

31 August 1914

*Recruiting begins for 1st
City (Pals) Battalion*

6 September 1914

First Battle of the Marne

19 October 1914

First Battle of Ypres

25 November 1914

*Recruitment begins for the 8th
and last Pals Battalion*

1915

25 April 1915

Allied landing at Gallipoli

7 May 1915

*Germans torpedo and
sink the Lusitania*

11 May 1915

Anti-German riots in Openshaw

31 May 1915

*First German Zeppelin
raid on London*

31 July 1915

*First prosecutions of Manchester
workers for going on strike*

20 December 1915

*Allies finish their evacuation of
and withdrawal from Gallipoli*

1916

24 January 1916

The British Government introduces conscription

21 February 1916

Battle of Verdun commences

23 February 1916

1st City Battalion deployed to Manchester Hill

31 May 1916

Battle of Jutland

4 June 1916

Brusilov Offensive commences

6 June 1916

Harold Wild attends a hearing at Hulme Town Hall to review his appeal for exception from military conscription

1 July 1916

First day of the Battle of the Somme with 57,000 British casualties

27 August 1916

Italy declares war on Germany

18 December 1916

Battle of Verdun ends

1917

6 April 1917

The United States declares war on Germany

9 April 1917

Battle of Arras

18 May 1917

Leaders of Manchester engineering union arrested

31 July 1917

Third Battle of Ypres (Passchendaele)

20 August 1917

Third Battle of Verdun

26 October 1917

Second Battle of Passchendaele

20 November 1917

Battle of Cambrai

7 December 1917

USA declares war on Austria-Hungary

18 December 1917

The Manchester Tank Bank

1918

3 March 1918

Russia and the Central Powers sign the Treaty of Brest-Litovsk

21 March 1918

Second Battle of the Somme

21 March 1918

The Manchester Hill offensive saw heavy causalities to the 1st and 2nd City Battalions

17 June 1918

George Davison killed in action

15 July 1918

Second Battle of the Marne

16 July 1918

First units of the US Army parade through Manchester

8 August 1918

Battle of Amiens, first stage of the Hundred Days Offensive

22 September 1918

The Great Allied Balkan victory

27 September 1918

Storming of the Hindenburg Line

8 November 1918

Armistice negotiations commence

9 November 1918

Kaiser Wilhelm II abdicates, Germany is declared a Republic

1924

12 July 1924

Cenotaph unveiled

ACKNOWLEDGEMENTS & PICTURE CREDITS

The following images are courtesy of:

Moss, Harold, ©Together Trust, page 39.
Wild, Harold, picture and extracts from his diary, 'The Diary
   of a Conscientious Objector, 1915-1919', courtesy of his
   daughter, Mrs Dorothy Spence, page 81.
Mrs Fisher, from the collection of Ken Fisher, page 114.
Jones, William Henry, receipt from Southern Cemetery, 1918,
   from the collection of Bob Jones, page 109.
Replica Cenotaph, *c.* 1924, from the collection of Nicola O'Niel,
   page 104.
Simpson, George Bradford, photograph *c.* 1918 and message
   from the Queen, 1999, from the collection of Andrew
   Simpson, page 122.

All remaining images courtesy of David Harrop.

INTRODUCTION

A CENTURY ON

The Great War has all but faded from living memory. Those men and women who played an active part in the conflict are now long gone and soon their children will have passed away too. In addition, some of the war memorials are at risk of being lost either through neglect and the passage of time or, in the case of a few, taken down and casually forgotten about. All of this does nothing for our perception of the First World War, which is now overlaid with misconceptions and omissions.

Clara, wearing the cap of the East Lancashire Regiment.

It starts with the photographs of men and women whose images are frozen in a moment in time, so we either see them as young and eager, staring back at us in ill-fitting uniforms or grey munitions overalls, or, more recently, as frail pensioners with faltering voices and walking sticks who were venerated as the last of their generation. But that is to forget that the majority of them lived full productive lives, contributed to their community, and got on with the daily demands of work, family and holidays long after the war had been consigned to the history books.

The Manchester's at
Haywards Heath,
undated postcard.

The MANCHESTERS are "holding their own" at Haywards Heath

And I doubt that they would always share the currently popularly held views of the war which pretty much are limited to the battlefields of France, the role of women in the munitions factories and the odd Zeppelin raid. They might well instead have pointed to the huge rise in the cost of living, the anger at perceived profiteering and defended the walkouts, strikes and demonstrations which rumbled through the four years of war.

All dressed up: possibly a picture for a serving soldier from his wife.

Two munitions workers.

Nor, I suspect, would the women engaged in the war effort have recognised that idea that they were welcomed into the workforce by a grateful nation, when in reality many experienced some discrimination, were often on lower wage rates than men doing similar work, and might have had to juggle their working life with the demands of bringing up a family.

Wedding party at Hough End Hall, May 1915.

The people of Manchester, Salford and the surrounding townships made a huge and willing contribution to the war effort, seen in the large numbers who volunteered for the Pals Battalions, the support given to local Red Cross hospitals and the numerous war funds, the sacrifices made in the homes and workplaces from Ancoats to Whalley Range, and, above all, in the personal sacrifices, like that of Mrs Bingle of Ardwick who lost three of her sons in the last year of the war, or Mr and Mrs Lunt of Chorlton-cum-Hardy who lost two sons in the space of twenty days in 1917.

Private Douglas Brown displaying the wound stripe.

So this is their story, told not just from the official reports and newspapers but also from letters and photographs and other personal items reflecting their work, recreation, putting food on the table and waiting for news from the Front.

Andrew Simpson
Manchester, 2017

1

MANCHESTER IN 1914

In the summer of 1914, Manchester, like many other cities across the country, was a place of contrasts. After a century and a half of economic growth it was a showcase of wealth and opportunity, with fine civic buildings, grand offices and prestigious warehouses, along with impressive railway stations and the Ship Canal, which united Manchester and Salford to the sea, and to the vast markets of the world.

Those decades of industrial enterprise are recorded for all to see across the city. In the Town Hall the names and coats of arms of the principle cities and countries which traded with

Piccadilly, early twentieth century.

Cross Street, early twentieth century.

Manchester are proudly displayed, while the day-to-day business of commerce operated in the bustling exchanges where commodities were bought and sold and commercial intelligence was shared. The city owed much to the textile industry but was also a centre of engineering and metal work, had its own deep shaft colliery and was home to countless smaller businesses specializing in everything from shipping insurance to tobacco manufacturers.

But less than a mile from all this glittering and solid evidence of success were the narrow streets, dark alleys and run-down parts of the city where 'poverty still busied itself'.[1] Manchester no longer had the slums which social observers Dr Kay and Frederick Engels had recorded in the early to mid nineteenth century, but there was still much that was grim and daunting.

The estimated total population of Manchester in 1914 was 731,830, and of that 210,494 were men between the ages of 15 and 45 years.

In 1904, a report on housing conditions drew attention to the 'many houses at present occupied [which] are unwholesome, because they have been badly built or are in need of repair. Such houses are frequently damp and cold. Many of them are old and dirty.' These suffered from a lack of basic sanitation and ventilation. Added to which, 'many

Market Street, early twentieth century.

St Peter's Square, early twentieth century.

of them have too many people living in them for the size and number of rooms' with rents 'on average very little lower than those paid for good houses in other parts of the town.'[2]

The report focused on parts of Ancoats, Ardwick, Hulme, and Chorlton-on-Medlock as well as Salford, where life at the turn of the century was still an unpredictable struggle to make ends meet and where unemployment, illness or the death of the main wage earner could pitch a family into destitution and the workhouse.

In 1911 a full 9 per cent of young people in Manchester between the ages of 10 and 14 were at work, which in the case of boys rose from just 1 per cent of those aged 10-12 to 30 per cent by their 14th birthday.

Looking at the list of charities is to appreciate just how many of the poor citizens of Manchester might be forced into asking for help. They ranged from the Ragged School, through to those for 'Destitute Women' and 'Inebriate Women', to a vast array of night shelters and asylums, as well as support groups for ex-prisoners and army veterans. In 1911 there were twenty-nine orphanages and homes for children across the city, along with the Open All-Night Children's Shelter, the St Vincent's Night Shelter and Home for Girls, and the fourteen centres operated by the Manchester and Salford Boys' and Girls' Refuges and Homes, which had been established in 1870 to provide a bed and meal for homeless young boys but quickly expanded to provide much more.[3] This included long-stay accommodation, training for work, as well as campaigning against the use of children as cheap labour and prosecuting neglectful parents.

The Royal Exchange, early twentieth century.

Royal Exchange, Manchester

Out on the Town

The city offered plenty in the way of attractions, ranging from open-air spaces to theatres, art galleries and cinemas. At the most basic level there were fifty-seven recreational grounds, from the small space in Chorlton-cum-Hardy which covered 2 acres with a children's play space and neatly laid flower beds broken by expanses of grass, to the Marie Louise Gardens which had over 4 acres and was described as a haven of tranquillity.

There were also the big parks. On the northern side of the city there was Heaton Park and Queen's Park, and at the southern end there was Platt Fields in Fallowfield and Alexandra Park in Moss Side.

The city boasted forty-two halls and assembly rooms offering everything from debates and lectures to music recitals. The discerning member of the public might sit one day in the grand surroundings of Manchester Town Hall and on another in the equally impressive Free Trade Hall on Peter Street, or travel across town by Corporation tram to the Independent Labour Party Hall in Gorton, and, on a whim, attend an event in the modest room of the Conservative Association on Burton Road in West Didsbury.

If you just wanted a night out there was a clutch of theatres or music halls, some bigger than others and some more prestigious. They might have included the Palace Theatre of Varieties on Oxford Street, the Hippodrome at Hulme or the Empire at Ardwick Green, and of these your fancy might well have been taken by 'What Price London? A revue in three scenes with a full company of 40 artistes' at the Empire during early July 1914.

Just two months later and with the war well underway the entertainment reflected the changed situation. The Hippodrome on Oxford Street staged 'a Grand Patriotic Scene: Soldiers of the King' while Belle Vue staged 'the Grand spectacle of the Battle of Kandahar'. During the war 'admission was 6d All Day Every Day'. These may have seemed quite tame compared to the attractions of the new picture houses. The Deansgate could seat 1,500 and through April 1914 their rivals on Market Street and Oxford Road were 'full to the doors with hundreds waiting for admission'.

Nicholas Road, Chorlton; one of the new suburbs, c. 1914.

With the uncertainty of war, work was rapidly diminishing, with some warehouses closing early and employers exploring short-time work. Many dockers were unable to get work and it was feared that the number of unemployed would increase daily.

Life expectancy amongst male manual workers was still low, and child labour was common in factories. Against this there was a steady rise in the cost of food and fuel, while wages failed to keep pace, culminating in a wave of strikes which swept the country. During 1911 and into 1912, carters, labourers in the engineering works, municipal workers and railwaymen all came out on strike in Manchester.

The city was also at the forefront of the campaign to extend the franchise which Mrs Annot Robinson – a well known and respected campaigner for women's rights and social justice for all – argued was about empowering women to allow 'them to have some share of political power', pointing out that in Manchester girls worked long hours for just six, seven, or eight shillings a week, and in the mackintosh trade wages sank below even that. 'It was this underpayment of girls that incited them to evil living. If women were given an opportunity of influencing the laws of the land matters would be mended.'[4]

Sandwiched between these extremes of wealth and poverty were those who made their living from a range of professional and clerical occupations and could afford to move to the more comfortable suburbs south of the city, which were close to the countryside but within easy reach of the city centre.

This exodus had started as early as the 1830s but began in earnest in the last quarter of the nineteenth century, made possible by the provision of mains water, improved sanitation and gas supplies and helped further by new railway links and the expansion of the Corporation tram network. It was a development which prompted the *Manchester Evening News* to report that 'the green fields of one summer are the roads and avenues of the next.'[5] These suburban houses ranged from the tall semi-detached properties which could be rented for between £25 and £35 a year down to the 'six shilling a week homes … modest four-roomed houses with plenty of breathing space'.[6]

These new communities were supported by their own shopping centres and a wide range of cultural and sporting activities, allowing the clerk or university lecturer the opportunity to relax in the evening or at weekends with a game of tennis, an operatic recital or debate the major issues of the day knowing that his children – after a day in any one of a number of private schools – could walk the nearby fields.

And the fields were still surprisingly close, allowing those commuters, along with many inner-city residents, access to the countryside within fifteen minutes of leaving Central Railway Station in the heart of Manchester. As for the political balance of the city, the last General Election before the war had returned two Liberal, two Labour and two Conservative MPs, while at the 1913 local elections, of the twenty seats contested the Conservatives won nine, the Liberals six, Labour four with one Independent, which represented a swing towards Labour and the Liberals.

Into this hurly-burly George and Nellie Davison were celebrating the first birthday of their son, Duncan. Nellie was born in Hulme in 1889, one of seven children. Her father was a dyer but briefly chanced his luck as a coal merchant before reverting back to his previous job. Her older brothers and sisters were engaged in a variety of occupations: two worked in the fabric trade, another was an iron turner and fitter and the eldest had a fish and chip business.

By 1911 the family were living in a three-room house on Percy Street in Hulme, bounded by City Road to the north and Stretford Road to the south.

George and Nellie Davison with their son, Duncan, c. 1915. George was in the Royal Field Artillery and was killed on 17 June 1918.

George was three years older than Nellie and was born in Harpurhey. His father was a solicitor's clerk and George, while working as a clerk, attended night school where he studied English, Latin, French and Euclid. It was hard work but, as he wrote to Nellie, 'your future happiness as well as my own depends largely on the results of my studies during the next few years.'[7]

Their marriage in 1908 was followed by the birth of their son and in the autumn of 1914 George, along with thousands of other men, volunteered for the army. There is no record of what George thought about the worsening international situation during June or July of that year, or about the German invasion of Belgium, the British ultimatum to Germany and the subsequent declaration of war, but Britain's entry into a continental war was not met with universal acclaim in Manchester.

The day before war was declared, there had been concerns expressed in letters to the *Manchester Guardian* about the dangers to trade, the advisability of being linked to Russia with its poor record on democracy and human rights, and the potential for a huge loss of life. Indeed, along with the moral issues of fighting there were those who felt Britain had more in common with Germany than either Russia or Serbia, and there were calls for Britain to remain neutral. The *Manchester Guardian* published a list of thirty churches and missions calling for just such a policy and reported meetings planned for Manchester to protest at the war, one of which was addressed by C.P. Scott, the editor of the paper.

Across the city the news that the country was at war was met with mixed feelings. In Salford historian Robert Roberts wrote,

Two members of the 6th Battalion of the Manchester Regiment in camp, 1910.

'the fourth of August 1914 caused no great burst of patriotic fervour among us. Little groups, men and women together (unusual, this), stood talking earnestly in the shop or at the street corner, stunned by the enormity of events.'[8]

Robert had been born Salford in 1905. His father was a 'brass finisher', which was a skilled job and marked him as part of the elite of the working force, while his mother ran a corner shop at 1 Waterloo Street, which was off Liverpool Street in Salford. The property consisted of just four rooms and was a typical corner shop, and as such Robert was well placed to pick up on the feelings of those who came into the shop, including those who expressed their disquiet.

Amongst sections of the Labour Movement there was the real concern that the war would divert attention from social needs, and that the only people who would benefit would be the armament firms.[9] This sentiment was matched by resolutions from trade unions like the Electrical Trades Union, which strongly protested against the war in Europe as a wanton and wilful waste of human life, 'which will be the cause of unparalleled misery and hardship to the workers of all countries'.[10]

This opposition never really went away and as the war deepened it maintained a constant, but the majority of the country swung

Mr Punch does propaganda.

THE TRIUMPH OF "CULTURE."

behind Britain's involvement. By September the Labour candidate in the Bolton by-election was unopposed by the other two parties because he was a wholehearted supporter of the war policy.[11]

A little over a month later the Labour MP for Manchester East, John Edward Sutton, speaking at a meeting in his constituency, commented that when the ultimatum was sent the Labour Party was practically unanimous in deciding to support the war and that the party would 'sink and fall with the government, bring the war to a successful issue'.[12]

The belief in fighting 'the war to a successful issue' was reflected in the surge of recruits joining up. In the two months after the outbreak of war, of the 280 Manchester undergraduates in the Officer Training Corps over 200 had taken commissions. But it was the formation of the Manchester Pals battalions which points to the popular support for the war.

The call for a battalion of Pals came from Lord Derby, speaking in Liverpool on 19 August, and was followed by a second appeal on the 27th. It rested on the simple idea that men who worked and lived together might well feel happier enlisting in the same unit. And it worked. The day after Lord Derby made his second appeal for volunteers a group of Manchester businessmen announced their intention to raise a battalion of men from the city's many warehouses and commercial districts, to be known as the Manchester Clerk's and Warehousemen's Battalion.

To assist in recruitment, those firms participating in the Pals scheme promised that employees enlisting in the two weeks following the appeal would be given four weeks' full pay, be guaranteed re-engagement on discharge from the army, and that their wives would receive half pay while in service. These were very real inducements to men whose civilian earnings far outweighed army pay, even given the allowances offered to married men with children.

There was a dramatic surge in men volunteering over the course of the next few months, and, despite problems in coping with the number trying to enlist in the first few days and a temporary fall off in volunteers during September, the rush to the colours resulted in the creation of eight Pals battalions in just five months.

It had taken just two days to raise the 1st City Battalion and the same again for the 2nd and 3rd battalions, and by 30 November the 7th and 8th were steadily progressing towards their full establishment.

Already many of those belonging to territorial units had volunteered for overseas service and during August and September the Manchester Regiment had raised three service battalions.

The surge in patriotic fervour was matched by the amounts of money donated to various relief funds, along with the growing number of men, women and children who volunteered for a wide variety of unpaid war work.

On 7 August a National Relief Fund was launched that received £1 million in donations within a week and which, by the end of the war, would total over £7 million. In Manchester, just a week after the launch, contributions amounted to £7,854, with donations ranging from £5,000 by Rylands & Sons Ltd to £10 from Mr Thomas Parker.[13]

These sums were matched by factories and other workplaces, leading the Secretary of the Manchester Relief Fund to record his thanks to the workers in Didsbury, West Didsbury and Withington for their kindness in assisting in raising locally the 'magnificent sum' of £162 2s 5d.[14] And there is no doubt that there was a pressing need for help in the opening weeks of the war. The *Manchester Guardian* reported that by 14 August there had been 1,000 applications for relief from reservists' wives.

There were also serious concerns about the growing numbers who found themselves out of work, prompting the Corporation to consider big public works schemes including the building of a new road south out of the city to Cheshire, through Burnage and Didsbury and then west to Cheadle, along with the creation of a new park in Chorlton, an extension to Heaton Park and 'something for Strangeways'.[15]

Unknown group of soldiers in Heaton Park, 1914.

These may well seem *ad hoc* solutions to pretty fundamental issues relating to a country entering a major continental war, and throughout the conflict there are plenty of examples where the government stumbled and bumbled along, but it was prepared enough to pass the Defence of the Realm Act (DORA) on 8 August alongside the Aliens Restriction Act, which required foreign nationals to register with the police and if necessary to be deported. Under the restrictions, 'an alien enemy must not travel beyond five miles from his registered address; must not retain possession of any motor-car, motorcycle or aircraft, any firearms, ammunition, explosives, any inflammable liquid, any contrivance for signalling, any carrier or home pigeon, cipher code or means of conducting secret correspondence.'

In Manchester the police required all aliens to complete a form and the details were then entered into a book. By 13 August the list consisted of 2,000 names and in the following weeks some of these people were arrested and removed for internment at Queensferry. They were taken by van to Victoria Station and some at least were chained together and their police escorts armed with rifles. The official justification was that they were prisoners of war but, to its credit, the *Manchester Guardian* condemned the practice as degrading.

Among those caught up in the events was Paul Arno Voight, a violin dealer living on Oxford Street. A registered alien, he was charged with failing to surrender a camera that belonged to his wife and which had been in the possession of a neighbour.

Egone Helmpacker, an Austrian musician, and his wife Estella were charged with not registering as aliens, which seems harsh given that he was actually an Italian who had been born in Trieste in Austria while his wife was born in Paris but was judged to be an enemy because of her marriage.

In addition, many foreign waiters were dismissed because it was judged their continued employment would upset public opinion, which also extended to forbidding hotel bands from playing German music.

During May 1915, anti-German feeling turned into physical attacks on properties owned by Germans. Shops on Oldham Road, Ashton Old Road, Bradford, Clayton and Openshaw were damaged while in Ancoats a crowd turned on five men of German nationality from the box-making works of H. Stevenson & Sons on Pollard Street. Many of those attacked were naturalised British citizens.

In readiness for the return of casualties from France and Belgium, the 2nd Western General Hospital had been established with its headquarters in the Central High School for Boys and Girls on Whitworth Street. On 6 August the War Office had mobilized the medical staff of the Royal Infirmary and commandeered four other public buildings in the city. A fortnight later, the *Manchester Guardian* reported that rapid progress had been made in equipping the school as a military base hospital, including the words 'Military Hospital' painted in large white letters on the outside wall fronting the street and the installation of a lift.[16]

Later in the month the Day Training College in Princess Street was also converted into a military hospital. Initially 520 beds were acquired with an option on an additional 630, but by the end of the war this had risen to 25,000 beds. These were spread out in small hospitals across the city and surrounding towns and ranged from public buildings like schools and church buildings to private houses. In Didsbury, along with buildings given by the Wesleyan College, there were a number of houses such as Woodlands which served throughout the conflict, two large Sunday school halls in Chorlton and much smaller properties pretty much everywhere.

The contingency plans had been agreed as far back as 1907 and involved the British Red Cross and St John's Ambulance providing a home hospital reserve, leaving the Royal Army Medical Corps to be deployed abroad.

As the War Office, Town Hall and the Red Cross began their preparations, so

Badge of the Burnley Volunteer Training Corps belonging to George Davison, who was briefly with them in 1914.

too did the Labour Movement, which, mindful that the war might erode pay and working conditions, formed the War Emergency Workers National Committee, tasked with defending the interests of working people. It was established on the day war broke out by the Labour Party, the Trades Union Congress and the Co-operative Movement, along with affiliated organisations and the Fabian Society, and during the next four years received daily reports on everything from rises in rents, the cost and quality of food, pensions and conditions in factories, the land as well as the railways, and extended to information about war babies, air raids and women's war service. Much of the correspondence came from local Labour and Trades Councils across the country, which set up their own local committees.

The proud record of the 2nd Western General Hospital: on 8 November 1914, ninety-one nursing staff were mobilized which eventually reached the figure of 691. During the course of the war 220,548 patients were treated and the total number of beds was 5,239.

In the city, the Manchester & District Workers (War Problems) Joint Committee consisted of the Manchester & Salford Trades and Labour Council, the Manchester & Salford Labour Party, Gorton Trades Council, the Engineering and Shipbuilding Trades Federation, the Building Industries Federation, the Women's Trade Union Council, the Manchester and Salford Women's Trade & Labour Council, the Manchester & Salford ILP, Manchester Salford & District Co-operative Societies, the Women's Co-operative Guilds, the Women's Citizen's Association, and the Women's War Interest Committee.

Food Vigilance Committees were also set up in Manchester and across the country to monitor prices and ensure local councils were enforcing regulations on both the price and the quality of food. They called meetings, distributed leaflets and, like the War Emergency Workers National Committee, pushed hard for more government intervention in regulating abuses thrown up by the war.

It proved to be an important move, as the cost of living continued to rise during the four years of the war, leading to accusations that some were profiteering at the expense of others.

By April 1918 there were over 1,000 allotments in the city, as well as over 2,000 under the control of the Foodstuffs Committee and 3,150 established by the Allotments Committee.

Robert Roberts remembered that the day after the war started there had been a rush of customers to his mother's shop, buying up all available stocks of sugar, flour, butter, bread, margarine and cheese, leading his mother to ration what there was to her regulars. But not being one to miss an opportunity she also dispatched her children in relays to join queues already formed outside Lipton's and Maypole Dairy and other groceries on the high road, purchasing 28lbs of margarine and 20lbs of sugar, which she promptly sold off in small lots at a penny a pound profit.[17]

This mass bulk buying resulted in the price of certain basic food stuffs doubling in two days, much pandemonium, and, in Salford at least, scenes not unlike a near riot with shop windows smashed and the police having to be called. Already the war offered up much that was new and challenging but was only the start of much to come.

NOTES

1 Roberts, Robert, *The Classic Slum: Salford Life in the First Quarter of the Century*, 1971, Pelican, 1973, p. 39
2 Housing Conditions in Manchester & Salford, a report prepared for the Citizens' Association for the Improvement of the Unwholesome Dwellings and Surroundings of People, T.R. Marr, Sherratt and Hughes, 1904, p. 4
3 Slater's Manchester, Salford & Suburban Directory 1911, pp 2138–2141
4 Women's Suffrage, The Conciliation Bill, Meeting in Alexandra Park, *Manchester Guardian*, 10 October 1910
5 A History of Manchester Suburbs, Chorlton, *Manchester Evening News*, 20 September 1901
6 Ibid.
7 Letter from George to Nellie, 17 May 1905
8 Roberts, Robert, *The Classic Slum*, 1973, Pelican, p. 187
9 Councillor W.T. Jackson, Secretary of the Manchester and Salford Labour Representation Committee, Labour Protest in Manchester, *Manchester Guardian*, 3 August 1914
10 The Attitude of Labour, *Manchester Evening News*, 3 August 1914

11 Bolton By-election, *Manchester Guardian*, 15 September 1914

12 The Labour Party, *Manchester Guardian*, 12 October 1914

13 Manchester Donations, *Manchester Guardian*, 13 August 1914

14 H.H. Bowden, Correspondence, *Manchester Guardian*, 8 October 1914

15 Relief Works, the Great South Road, *Manchester Guardian*, 27 August 1914

16 Manchester and the War, the Base Hospital, *Manchester Guardian*, 22 August 1914

17 Ibid., p. 186

2

ADJUSTING TO WAR

The transformation from peacetime to war was swift and all-pervasive. On 5 August the *Manchester Guardian* reported that an estimated 30,000 Manchester and Salford men would receive the 'call to arms', which included the men of the Naval Reserve, the Army Reserve, the Special Reserve and the Territorial Force. The City Council was to lose 1,292 men to the army, the city's police force approximately 100 and some of the larger warehouses also lost part of their workforce.

Just like the assurances that were made to those enlisting in the first Pals battalions, some employers, including the Corporation, promised to keep jobs open, and in the case of the Watch Committee, to recommend that allowances be paid to the wives and children of the reservists.

Embroidered silk postcard with the badge of the Manchester Regiment.

1st City Battalion in Heaton Park, 1914.

In contrast to the general mix of excitement and trepidation, one newspaper reported that reservists reporting for duty at the headquarters of the 8th Ardwick Battalion of the Manchester's had routinely gone about their work as though they were preparing for an annual training camp, despite a large and excited crowd which had gathered outside.

By the end of the first full day of the war practically all the physicians and surgeons at the Manchester Royal Infirmary had been mobilized for service at the new military hospital on Whitworth Street, and by 10 September the first six frontline territorial battalions of the Manchester Regiment had left Southampton for service abroad.

During August they had been based at Hollingworth Lake near Rochdale, and the close proximity to the city meant that relatives could make the journey out to visit. Similarly, the first two Pals battalions set up camp at Heaton Park, followed by other battalions.

At first the troops had been accommodated in tents but these were replaced by huts which were supplemented by various

*In Heaton Park
with some of the
Manchester's, 1914.*

'comforts'. The Corporation agreed the creation of recreational facilities and the YMCA set up recreation tents, leading the Revd W.H. Neat of Whalley Range to appeal for 'interesting books and games, such as chess, draughts and dominoes [which] the friends of the soldiers could send by tramcar addressed to the YMCA Recreation Tents, Heaton Park.'

In those early months other Pals battalions like the 3rd City Battalion were temporarily placed at White City, while the 6th, 7th and 8th ended up at the seaside in Morecombe, while many had at first been billeted at home, making their way each day to the training centres.

By then the first rush of volunteers had fallen away. During the spring of 1915 enlistment across the country was averaging 100,000 a month, while in Manchester a recruitment drive in the middle of May resulted in just 850 men joining up, which was only a little more than one-seventh of the reinforcement that had been hoped for.[1]

This was not judged enough to match the casualties returning from the battlefronts, so as early as August 1914 the height restrictions were lowered and in May of the following year the upper age limit was raised from 38 to 40.

It made sense to explore just how many men were out there who were fit for military service and so, on 15 July 1915,

Parliament passed the National Registration Act, which set out the means by which 'a register shall be formed of all persons, male and female, between the ages of 15 and 65 (not being members of His Majesty's naval forces or His Majesty's regular or territorial forces)'.[2]

The registration was undertaken in a similar way to a census, with some 29 million forms issued across England and Wales. But unlike the census where the householder was responsible for filling in the form, under the Registration Act it was the responsibility of each man and woman to complete their own form.

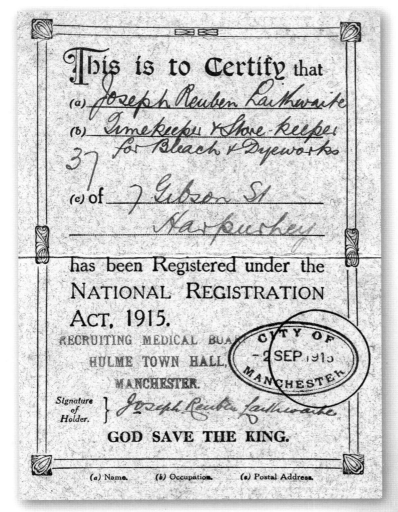

Registration card belonging to Joseph Reuben Laithwaite, September 1915.

R 50.

ARMY RESERVE B.

VOLUNTARILY ATTESTED MAN.

CERTIFICATE OF EXEMPTION.

Certificate of Exemption.

The returned forms were collected in mid-August and compiled by the local authority, the statistics being passed on to the Register General. It showed there were almost five million men of military age who were not in the forces, of which over a million were in scarce or essential occupations.

One of those who registered at the Town Hall was Mr Joseph Reuben Laithwaite, who gave his occupation as a 'timekeeper and store keeper for a Bleach and Dyeworks'. In 1915 he was 39 years old and lived with his wife, young daughter and father-in-law in Hapurhey. He enlisted under the Derby or Group Scheme, which was introduced in November 1915 as a half-way house between voluntary enlistment and compulsion. It offered the opportunity for men to enlist but defer their call up to a later date.

A total of 215,000 men enlisted while the scheme was on and another 2,185,000 chose to delay their enlistment (those who were on the deferred list were given a grey or khaki armband with a red crown). But this still left a large pool of potential recruits who had not shown a willingness to serve, and so in January 1916 the Military Service Act was passed introducing conscription.

3,000 employees from Manchester Corporation Tramways enlisted during the war. Of these 310 lost their lives and are remembered on memorial plaques at the remaining bus garages.

The Act required that all men between the ages of 18 to 41 were liable for service in the army unless they were married, widowed with children, in the Royal Navy, a minister of religion or in a reserved occupation. Later, in May 1916, married men were also made liable for conscription and two years later the upper age limit was raised to 51.

But it appears that Mr Laithwaite was passed over. There is no record of him enlisting or serving in the armed forces and he appears to have died in Heywood in 1953, having reached the ripe age of 77.

Those who did not wait for conscription included the 200 men from Little Italy who returned to their home country when Italy joined the war on the side of the Allies in May 1915.[3]

Little Italy was situated behind Great Ancoats Street in a small area bounded by Gun Street, Bengal Street and Jersey Street. There had been a small group of Italian businessmen and their families in the city from the early nineteenth century, but from the 1860s a much larger group arrived in Manchester looking for a better life. By the beginning of the twentieth century the community was well established, with its own cultural associations. Many of the inhabitants worked in the local mills and some branched out into enterprises of their own.

Harold Moss of the 15th Battalion of the Lancashire Fusiliers was killed on 17 March 1916.

Along with those who returned to fight in Italy, those who had been born in Britain volunteered for the British Army. Their contribution was recorded on a simple marble memorial which was placed beside the Cenotaph in 1925. It carried the inscription 'The Italian Comrades' and while it was removed during the Second World War it has since been returned and lies at the foot of the Cenotaph in its new location outside the Town Hall.

Equally important but often overlooked was the contribution of those young men in the care of the Manchester and Salford Boys' and Girls' Refuges and Homes. Many had had a shaky start in life. Some had been rescued from the streets and others had gone into the care of the charity when, for a variety of reasons, they could no longer be looked after at home.[4]

One of these was Harold Moss, who was admitted to the charity in 1906. Here he stayed until he was 14, when he began work in a drapery shop as an apprentice. He enlisted at the beginning of the war and was sent to France with the 15th Battalion of the Lancashire Fusiliers. He was killed on 17 March 1916, aged just 20.

The departure of so many young men was not the only obvious change to life in the city. The imposition of blackout regulations proved both irksome and dangerous. In November 1914 regulations under the Defence of the Realm Act concerning sky signs, which until now had affected only London, were extended to the whole of the country. At the same time, it became compulsory to have blinds in railway carriages drawn down between dusk and dawn.

The following year a series of further Lighting Orders were introduced, which ranged from painting the tops of street lamps to reducing the lighting in tramcars and buses to a point where there was just enough light necessary to collect the fares.

The degree to which all this was effective varied, but according to one newspaper a walk through the main streets of the city revealed that the new regulations had been successful. On Oxford Street, Deansgate and Market Street the use of opaque blinds, shaded lamps and even blue electric bulbs had darkened buildings, while out in the suburbs the rush to make blackout curtains had almost exhausted supplies in some shops.[5] Unfortunately, the blackout resulted in an increase in the number of street accidents and the police were forced to issue warnings about cars speeding on darkened roads.

The Defence of the Realm Act effected almost all aspects of ordinary life. The original Act had focused on ensuring the security of the nation's sea ports and railways, prohibiting links with the enemy and making civilians subject to military courts, along with the compulsory requisition of

On the death of Harold Moss: 'We were very grieved to hear of his death. We shall miss him very much, but it is a comfort to know he has died as he always tried to live, doing his duty and helping others.' Mrs Howarth of the Manchester and Salford Boys' and Girls' Refuges and Homes writing about Harold, who had been in her care.

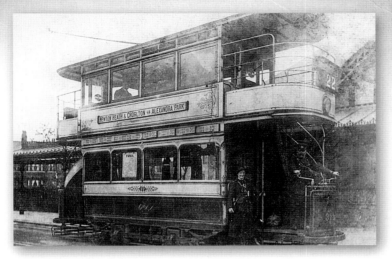

Wartime tram, complete with 'clippie' and blackout blind.

factories and their output. It was amended six times and was used to introduce a series of controls to support the war effort. These included rationing, restrictions on public house opening hours, and censorship. Other orders included banning people from loitering near bridges, lighting bonfires and flying kites (objects thrown from a bridge could derail a train, and a bonfire or even a kite with a lamp attached might be used to attract a Zeppelin).

Equally intrusive was the introduction of the two Munitions of War Acts in 1915 and 1916, which made strikes and lock-outs illegal and instead replaced them with a system of statutory arbitration covering everything from disputes over pay and conditions to the right of workers to leave a workplace, and for companies to make 'excess profits arising from increased volume of work'.

The original Act had been limited in its definition of munitions work but in 1916 this was extended to cover the manufacture and repair of almost everything 'intended or adapted for use in war'.[6] According to the deliberations of the arbitration panels this included such things as the manufacture of insulating materials in the construction of electrical machinery, and the repair of railway wagons belonging to a colliery.

It followed that 'so far reaching are the efforts of the belligerents in this war that there is hardly anything on the earth, in the air or in the waters that could not under some circumstances be described as an article capable of use in war.[7] This extended to the manufacture of a whole battery of materials and machinery, along with the supply of light, heat, water, power and tramway facilities and even the construction of houses to accommodate munitions workers and even the repair of fire engines, prompting one arbitration panel to consider whether firemen were munitions workers.

The country had become one vast arsenal for the war effort and inevitably disputes arose between workers on the one side and employers and the State on the other. Just months after the original Act was passed the first prosecutions in Manchester took place on a Saturday at the end of July, when thirty-two workmen at Craven Brothers in Reddish were brought before a munitions tribunal for 'engaging in a strike over wages and conditions of employment'. This was followed a fortnight later when fourteen men from Dempsters, a gas plant manufacturer in Miles Platting, were summoned for similar offences. The verdicts were swift and uncompromising, if lenient. The 'Craven 32' were fined 2s 6d each with the costs of the proceedings which amounted to £3 3s divided among them, while the fourteen from Miles Platting were subject to a range of fines from 5s to 10s.

At the outbreak of the war plans had been set in motion to recruit 5,000 special constables who would be divided into commands of fifty men led by a 'leader'. By 21 August twenty leaders had been enrolled and there had been 200 applications to join the force; such was the interest in volunteering that it was reported that by November the Special Police Reserve had reached their target of 5,000. The following year the Chief Constable doubled the hours of the special constables. Instead of one tour a week of four hours they were required to perform two tours of duty of four hours each. This was to ensure a sufficient supply for the evening stretching into the early morning, and had been prompted by the increasing number of regular constables who had enlisted and the impossibility of getting suitable men who were not already involved in other war work.[8]

Some of the specials, however, viewed aspects of their work as mundane and even as unnecessary. Writing to the *Manchester Guardian* in February 1915, 'Special Constable' could see little point in his patrolling Mount Street, Exchange Street and St Anne's Street when there was always a policeman on point duty well within a hail.[9]

Such are the little events which make for the bigger picture, and part of that picture in the early months of 1915 revolved around drunkenness, which appeared to justify the decision in March 1915 by the military authorities to order a restriction on the opening hours of pubs across the Western Command, which included Manchester. According to the order, 'all licensed premises (whether for the consumption on or off the premises) shall only be opened on weekdays between the hours of 10.30 a.m. and 10 p.m. and on Sundays between 12.30 and 2.30 p.m. and between the hours of 6.30 p.m. and 9 p.m.'

The justification rested on reports of the high level of drunkenness amongst soldiers and workmen in the mornings and later led to further restrictions on opening hours, treating and buying rounds, and a reduction in the strength of spirits. Many in the licensing trade suspected the hand of the temperance movement and said as much. In turn the movement, feeling emboldened, called for a complete ban on alcohol for the duration of the war.

In the first few months there were mixed reports about the impact on trade and while the *Manchester Guardian* conceded that in the majority of cases the regulations had lessened the profits of publicans, it had also ferreted out examples where businesses in the city centre had stayed the same or even improved, as some who would normally have had a drink after returning home chose to 'fill up' before catching their tram or train.[10]

Another change introduced to assist the war effort was British Summer Time (BST), which came into force in 1916. The advantages of an extra hour of daylight seemed obvious both in the saving on artificial light and the consumption of coal. The Gas Department of the Manchester Corporation estimated that there would be a fall in the consumption of gas and coal which was all to the good given that the year before the price had been increased in an effort to cut usage and so save reserves. This hadn't worked and so it was reasoned an extra hour of daylight would help. However, the impact was questionable because, as the Gas Department reported in October, while there had been a fall in the use of coal and gas in the evenings after the start of BST, it was counteracted by a rise during the day.

Before the war, many small porcelain souvenirs graced the mantelpieces and glass-fronted cabinets of many Manchester homes. These were bought as a reminder of a cherished seaside holiday or of a day trip (ranging from a replica of a thatched cottage to a teapot and almost anything between) but with the outbreak of war manufacturers began creating designs influenced by the war. Some of the most popular were tanks and ambulance cars, which carried the coat of arms of the city in which they were sold. The author's favourite is a figurine of HMS *Manchester*, which was made by the Arcadian company of Stoke-on-Trent who, in peacetime, turned out figurines, local museum antiques and functional items like ring trees, stamp boxes and pin trays. What marks HMS *Manchester* out as unique is that while there have been three ships bearing the name of the city, none served in the Great War!

The same preoccupation with war themes was inevitably reflected in the picture postcards of the time. Some of the most humorous were based on risqué situations or suggestions, like Tom's card to Alice which carried the picture of a pair of long laced pyjama bottoms with the message 'Meet me To-night in Dreamland [but] Not in these'. Others edged towards the romantic and many more conjured up idealised scenes of lovers who had been separated but now were reunited.

Beside these were those mourning the loss of a loved one, be it a sweetheart, a husband or a father. Some of them may strike a modern reader as mawkish but there is no denying the force of cards like the one portraying a mother and child on a flight of stairs and the question, 'Mother, why doesn't Daddy come home?'

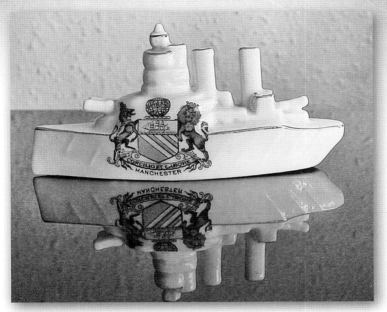

HMS Manchester *crested china.*

A large number of cards featured photographs of soldiers in uniform, some in groups, and others with a sweetheart, wife or family group. The cards ranged from commercially produced scenes of a training camp or Red Cross Hospital, images of battered Belgium towns, patriotic calls to participate in war savings schemes and appeals from charities, to very personal ones taken in a studio and meant for a limited circulation. Some of the most beautiful are the embroidered ones, many of which were made in France and carry designs of flowers or a regimental badge.

The cost of sending letters remained low while those from the Front were sent back free, and, although a letter was always better than a postcard, the army provided the field-service postcard as a quick and easy way of making contact with home. The card contained a series of pre-printed messages ranging from 'I am quite well', 'I have been admitted to hospital', 'I have received your letter/telegram/parcel' to 'Letter follows at first opportunity'. All that was required was to cross out the comments that were not relevant.

> The cost of sending letters to troops was charged at 1*d* for an ounce letter; the cost was the same no matter where it was addressed.

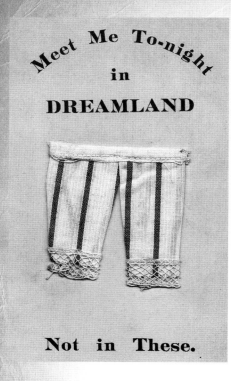

Meet Me To-night in **DREAMLAND**

Not in These.

NOTHING is to be written on this side except the date and signature of the sender. Sentences not required may be erased. If anything else is added the post card will be destroyed.

[Postage must be prepaid on any letter or post card addressed to the sender of this card.]

I am quite well.

~~I have been admitted into hospital~~

~~{ sick ~~ and am going on well.

~~{ wounded }~~ ~~and hope to be discharged soon.~~

~~I am being sent down to the base.~~

~~I have received your { letter dated~~ _____

~~telegram~~ _____

~~parcel~~ _____

Letter follows at first opportunity.

~~I have received no letter from you~~

~~{ lately~~

~~{ for a long time.~~

Signature only } *William*

Date *28-10-17*

W: W3497293. 39244. 8000m. 9716. C. & Co., Grange Mills, S.W.

Above left: 'Don't care for stripes, do you darling, I like them plain myself'.

Above right: Field-service postcard.

In addition to the field-service postcard there were the Green envelopes or Honour envelopes, so-called because the sender agreed that what was inside was a purely personal message which did not require the censor to read it. To make sure that this was clearly understood, to the left of the address under the heading 'Note' was the clear injunction that 'correspondence in this envelope need not be censored Regimentally. The Contents are liable to examination at the Base. The following Certificate must be signed by the writer: I certify on my honour that the contents of this envelope refer to nothing but private and family matter.'

George Davison preferred the conventional letter which, while often short on detail, regularly arrived at the family home.

The war saw a reduction in the number of deliveries to three a day, but given the huge transformation the conflict had brought about this was perhaps a small inconvenience.

NOTES

1 Recruitment campaign in Manchester, *Manchester Guardian*,
   29 May 1915
2 First clause of the National Registration Act 1915
3 Anthony Rea, *Manchester's Little Italy*, Neil Richardson, 1988 and
   www.ancoatslittleitaly.com/index.html
4 Archives of the Together Trust
5 New Lighting Order in Manchester, *Manchester Guardian*,
   11 January 1916
6 1916 Act S 9 (1), p. 82
7 Mr Justice Atkin, the Shaw *vs* Lincoln Wagon Company, 1916,
   quoted on p. 6
8 Special Constables, Two Weekly Beats, *Manchester Guardian*,
   28 June 1915
9 Citizen Police: First Week on the Active List, *Manchester
   Guardian*, 15 February 1915
10 Drink Restrictions, *Manchester Guardian*, 10 April 1915

The last letters from George to Nellie Davison

During 1918 George Davison wrote regular letters home to his wife Nellie and son Duncan. Even after he arrived in France he wrote every few days, and like many of his letters they were a mix of requests for news from home, reassurances about his own safety and snippets about friends he had encountered at the Front. On 2 June he told Nellie that he didn't need any money or tobacco to be sent but 'a little spearmint occasionally and a tube of toothpaste once every month would be very welcome.'

A week later he made a rare reference to the fighting when, having attended a church service, he recorded that 'a church service of half an hour close to the line, where voices are occasionally drowned by the heavier note of Gunfire carries an account of conviction not otherwise attainable.'

His final letters talk of the irritations of moving around the Front, including the loss of personal equipment and the varying quality of the accommodation. On 15 June he wrote, 'You would be surprised to see some of our living places – at present we have an excellent dugout about 20 feet below the surface. It has however two drawbacks – poor ventilation and only artificial (candle) light. Compared to some it is a Palace.'

And this was where he died on 17 June, when the dugout received a direct hit. All three men in the dugout were killed and according to the Royal Engineers who inspected the position, 'it was not considered safe to recover the bodies'. The dugout was filled in and is marked as the resting place of George and his comrades.

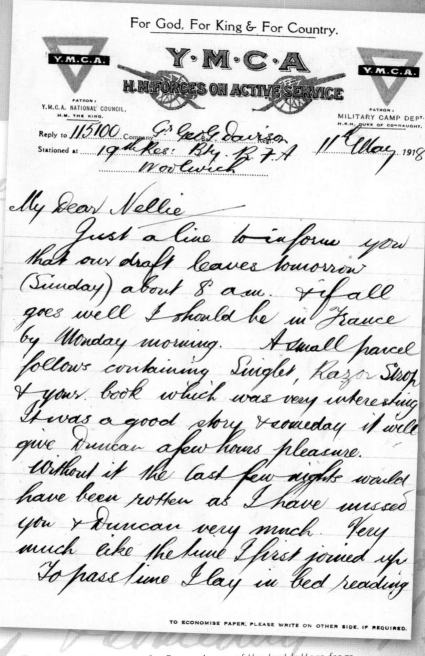

Y·M·C·A

H.M. FORCES ON ACTIVE SERVICE

Y.M.C.A.   Y.M.C.A.

PATRON:
Y.M.C.A. NATIONAL COUNCIL,
H.M. THE KING.

PATRON:
MILITARY CAMP DEPT.
H.R.H. DUKE OF CONNAUGHT.

Reply to 115100 Company Gr Geo G Davison Bat. Regt. 11 May 1918

Stationed at 19th Res: Bty. B 7 A
Woolwich

My Dear Nellie

Just a line to inform you
that our draft leaves tomorrow
(Sunday) about 8 a.m. & if all
goes well I should be in France
by Monday morning. A small parcel
follows containing Singlet, Razor Strop
& your book which was very interesting
It was a good story & someday it will
give Duncan a few hours pleasure.
Without it the last few nights would
have been rotten as I have missed
you & Duncan very much. Very
much like the time I first joined up
To pass time I lay in bed reading

TO ECONOMISE PAPER, PLEASE WRITE ON OTHER SIDE, IF REQUIRED.

*'Our draft leaves tomorrow for France': one of the last letters from
George Davison to his wife Nellie, 11 May 1918.*

3

DIGGING DEEP

Of all the many charitable activities which made a contribution to the war effort, the work of the Red Cross and St John Ambulance stand out for special consideration, not only because of their role in caring for the sick and wounded returning from the battlefronts but also because they highlight the degree to which local communities came together.

In 1909 the War Office had issued its 'Scheme for the Organisation of Voluntary Aid in England and Wales' in recognition that in the event of a major continental war the armed forces would need help in dealing with the large number of casualties. The scheme established Voluntary Aid Detachments (VAD) drawn from both male and female volunteers who would be trained by the St John Ambulance Association and organised by the British Red Cross Society. This was followed in August 1914 by the formation of the Joint War Committee between the Red Cross and St John Ambulance, which organised volunteers and professional staff both at home and on the battlefields.

In Manchester a large part of the work was carried out by the East Lancashire Branch of the British Red Cross, which very early in the war described its role as 'a voluntary organisation supported by public subscriptions … to supplement the medical services of the army and navy and to supply comforts to soldiers and sailors in addition to those provided by the authorities.' It had been formed in 1910 and at the outbreak of war had a total

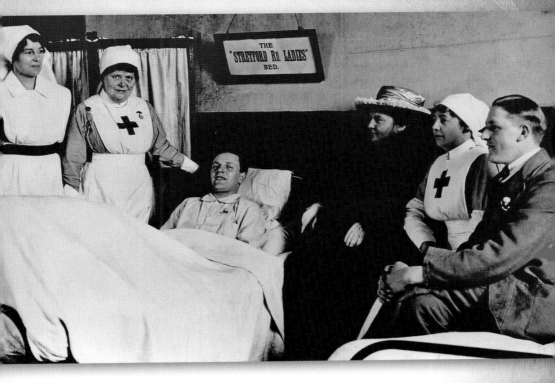

THE "STRETFORD Rd. LADIES" BED.

membership of 3,000 men and 1,000 women, along with forty Comforts Sections.

Willow Bank Hospital, Moss Lane East, 1919.

In the first few weeks of August 1914 it experienced a surge of interest from the general public, leading the branch to report that at its headquarters in the YMCA on Peter Street it had taken the efforts of the County Director and numerous staff to cope with the continuous stream of callers and with the postal and telephone inquiries, with offers of assistance pouring in on all sides.[1]

In the first three months of the war the branch was responsible for seventeen auxiliary hospitals across the city and in the neighbouring areas of Salford and Trafford, offering a total of 657 beds, with another 1,100 'beds almost ready' and, in conjunction with the St John Ambulance, was managing twelve more hospitals in the surrounding towns.[2] All of this represented a huge commitment on the part of local communities, who not only supplied the staff but provided comforts, entertainment and considerable financial support.

51

In the first few months of the war there was some confusion amongst the public about the role of the VAD. The term VAD applied both to a detachment and to an individual volunteer who could be involved in a variety of tasks from nursing to cooking, working in the laundry or as a typist, telephonist or driver. Their uniforms reflected both their roles and their ranks: nursing staff wore a pale blue dress, cooks a pale brown, quartermasters were in grey while commandants wore scarlet.

Along with the confusion as to the work of the VADs there were those who questioned whether they should be referred to as nurses given that some had only basic medical training. A Mr Bigwood of Whitelow Road in Chorlton-cum-Hardy, writing to the *Manchester Guardian* in January 1915, also suggested that young men employed as orderlies were avoiding military service, adding that they should not be allowed to wear a uniform which resembled that of a soldier.[3] It was a serious accusation and one which chimed with the handing out of white feathers to men deemed to be shirking enlistment. It prompted a swift reply from Mr Christopher, an orderly at the hospital, who stated that the Red Cross hospitals were a training ground for a lot of the VAD members who were awaiting to enlist.[4]

The Chorlton-cum-Hardy hospital was in the large Sunday school of the local Baptist church, which was offered up by the congregation and was converted into 'a ward of 31 beds, kitchens, mess room, dispensary pack stores, linen stores, matron's room and office.' Later the Methodist church gave up their large Sunday school, and at least one private home close by was also handed over to the Red Cross. This was the pattern across the city, with hospitals being set up in converted public buildings and residential properties.

The East Lancashire Branch in its appeal for sites made it clear that 'the War Office prefers that anyone giving such hospitality should undertake to receive not less than ten patients.' Typical of these was Woodlawn in Didsbury, which had been lent to the Red Cross by the executors of the late J. Broome and was a large house in 'one of the healthiest residential suburbs of Manchester and surrounded by extensive grounds.'[5]

The Red Cross was quite resourceful in their search for suitable premises and the Willow Bank Hospital in Moss Side was typical. It had been three grand private houses, which the society rented and converted with some structural changes into 'one Hospital containing 18 wards, operating theatre, mess room, billiard room, pack stores, matron's room, linen room, kitchen, and bathroom.'[6] The properties are still there today, located between Upper Lloyd Street and Monton Street, and while they have long ago lost their impressive gardens they still have a hint of their past grandeur.

Willow Bank also offers an interesting insight into the way that society promoted the voluntary contributions of individuals, workplaces and businesses by placing a notice above the beds referring to those who had made a donation, like the employees of H. Potter & Co. who had supplied a bed. The company made baby linen and was located on Moss Lane East on the corner with Cross Cliffe Street. There were also listings for the employees of Messrs Padden and the Gibbson Company, as well as individuals like Miss Hunter and Mr Rowe.

CHORLTON-CUM-HARDY RED CROSS HOSPITAL

The people of Chorlton-cum-Hardy did much to support their own Red Cross Hospital, subscribing the money to equip it and providing many extra luxuries for the patients over and above the guidelines laid down by the War Office.

During 1914 and 1915, 159 volunteers worked at the hospital, many drawn from just eighteen families. They were a mixed bunch, ranging from Mrs Fannie Jane Barlow, a mother of two whose husband was an accountant, Miss Bates, whose father was a coal porter and who worked in a laundry, Sidney Bolt, who was employed in his father's shop and Miss Ethel Bedford, who was a school teacher.

All were engaged in November 1914 when the hospital was opened. Mrs Barlow, who by then was 42 years old, served as a nurse, Miss Bates and Miss Bedford worked in the kitchen, while Mr Bolt was an orderly

Some of the volunteers would also be touched by the tragedy of the war. Thomas Ellwood, who served on the committee, lost his son Thomas in February 1917, as did the housekeeper, Mrs Emma Worlidge, whose son Oswald was also killed in 1917.

Christmas at Willow Bank.

A. CENTRAL

At one auxiliary hospital 137 men were treated between November 1914 and August 1915. Of these 117 were British, one was Canadian and another Australian and there were also eighteen Belgians. They had been wounded in France, Belgium and Gallipoli.

Most men were suffering from bullet or shrapnel wounds, some had been gassed, or suffered from frostbite, tetanus or rheumatism. Their stay varied from between two and three months and they would have been a common sight in the parks, streets and public buildings in their blue hospital uniforms. Many were photographed by commercial photographers, who sold the images on to picture postcard companies.

The work of the Red Cross extended beyond the care of the sick and wounded in the auxiliary hospitals. Early in the war volunteers placed their cars into a transport service for the 2nd Western General Hospital and between August 1914 and May 1915 moved 22,000 'wounded men from the ambulance trains to the base hospital and from the base hospital to the auxiliary home hospitals in East Lancashire and Cheshire.'[7]

Less well known today was the work the Red Cross volunteers did in the munitions factories, where they worked in shifts ready

Willow Bank men in hospital blues.

Badge awarded to support workers at Dover House on Oxford Road.

to deal with everything from an explosion to accidents with boiling vitriol and molten metal.

The Society also maintained a workshop – Dover House on Oxford Road. The Manchester War Hospital Supply Workroom was established in June 1916 to provide supplies ranging from bandages to arm slings. The work was undertaken by a group of volunteers assisted by girls from Manchester High School, who attended each afternoon and assisted in a variety of ways.

The Red Cross and St John Ambulance were also involved in providing 'comforts' for the men at the Front and recovering in hospitals through regular appeals for books and magazines to entertainments staged in hospitals. Typical of these was the one reported on by the *Manchester Guardian* during Christmas 1916 at Woodlawn in Didsbury. All six wards had been decorated by the patients and a large laurel wreath bearing an

Dover House had three workshops which produced surgical equipment and hospital garments. One room was devoted to the manufacture of slippers, another produced bandages, dressings and surgical swabs, and the third made a new type of arm sling known as the 'Davies sling', which had originated in the workhouse.

inscription was hung in one of the larger wards to the memory of those who had died.[8] On Christmas Day an NCO from each ward dressed up as Father Christmas, handing out 'a parcel of useful presents and other good things, followed after dinner by a whist drive' and songs and dances. Then on Boxing Day evening there was a ping-pong tournament with an evening concert.

By the end of the war thousands of people had made some contribution towards the work of the Red Cross and St John Ambulance. Most were content with knowing that their work had made a difference, but for some there would be official recognition in the form of a medal or an honour.

As for the auxiliary hospitals, many of these temporary facilities for wounded servicemen vanished as swiftly as snow in the winter sun. A few became permanent hospitals or rest homes; some were adapted into schools, but most reverted to their peacetime use. The remaining equipment was put up for auction and anyone having claims against the hospital for articles lent or goods supplied were asked to make an application in writing.

On 21 May 1919 the auction took place of 'the excellent furniture and equipment of what had been the Auxiliary Military Hospital on Wilbraham Road in Chorlton-cum-Hardy', including:

> 70 capital iron combination bedsteads, wool, hair and fibre mattresses, 550 blankets, 636 sheets, 20 counterpanes, 270 towels, a large quantity of pillows bolsters, 178 pyjama suits, 90 pairs of socks and other underwear, 40 chairs, three capital wardrobes, four dressing stands with mirrors, 50 bedside lockers, capital carpets, two pairs of scales buckets, pans brushes, screens, medical galvanised battery, Swift Typewriter and other property along with an upright iron grand pianoforte.[9]

And on the same day, just down the road at Bradshaw's Garage, the Red Cross put up for sale a number of motor ambulances without any reserve price.

So complete was the transition back to peacetime use that within a couple of generations the existence of these hospitals had all but faded from local knowledge, and today it can be quite a surprise to discover that one had existed just down the road and dispensed such essential care.

But what is lost or forgotten can be rediscovered, and so it was with the Wesleyan silver cup that had lain at the back of a cupboard for decades. It had been presented to the Chorlton Methodist Church in 1917 as a thank you from some of the men recovering in the converted Sunday school. It carried the simple inscription, 'Presented to the Wesleyan Church by the Wounded Soldiers of the Wesleyan Schools Hospital Xmas 1917'.

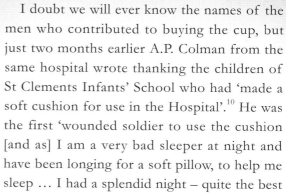

I doubt we will ever know the names of the men who contributed to buying the cup, but just two months earlier A.P. Colman from the same hospital wrote thanking the children of St Clements Infants' School who had 'made a soft cushion for use in the Hospital'.[10] He was the first 'wounded soldier to use the cushion [and as] I am a very bad sleeper at night and have been longing for a soft pillow, to help me sleep … I had a splendid night – quite the best since I have been wounded', concluding he was glad that 'they are learning while they are young to find out that we can get real pleasure by helping and doing things for other people … I hope as they grow older they will always remember this cushion.'

Silver cup presented to the Methodist church, 1917.

Together, the letter and the cushion reflect that greater effort on the part of local community to dig deep and help other people during the war. It began with the launch of the National Relief Fund on 6 August 1914 'for the relief of the inevitable distress which must be bravely dealt with in the coming days.' The Fund raised £1 million within its first week and by the end of the war subscriptions to the Fund amounted to nearly £7 million.[11] In Manchester, as elsewhere, the newspapers carried regular reports on the working of the Fund, its distribution and those who had donated. On 24 August the *Manchester Guardian* reported that the contribution from the city to the National Relief Fund had reached the sum of £35,468 – of which the Co-operative Wholesale Society had given £10,000.

The national money was distributed back down through agencies with the express purpose of spending rather than hoarding it. As early as October 1914 one fifth of the funds subscribed had been allotted for distribution.

And the well of local and national giving was deep. In all, approximately 18,000 charities were established during the Great War, providing help for refugees, prisoners of war, disabled servicemen and families at home, and continuing after the war with the erection of remembrance monuments in villages, towns and cities across the country.

The papers continued to carry listings for comforts organisers and there were appeals for a wide range of comforts for the troops. At the start of the war Mrs W.A. Fraser of The Elms, Seymour Grove, Old Trafford had given her address as the contact for sending 'gifts of woollen mittens' for men of the 3rd City Battalion of the Manchester Regiment, who were based at White City.

Of these 'comforts' the most popular were those associated with tobacco and cigarettes, with regular 'Fag Days' during which the population was urged to buy a flag 'in the cause of our gallant wounded heroes. Every penny paid for a flag today means 14 fags for our wounded men in hospitals, ambulance trains, both at home and abroad.'[12]

Alongside the push for subscriptions for a range of charities came the official appeals for money to finance the war. In 1914 the government had embarked on a scheme of war loans from the general public but these failed to appeal to everyone and so in 1916 they introduced war savings certificates, which were only available to individuals and with special permission to charities

OUT FOR VICTORY.

BRITISH WORKING MAN: "Give us another fifteen-an'-sixer, miss, to take home to the old girl."

Savings card.

The Manchester Tank, crested china, possibly bought during Tank Bank Week, 1917.

and provident societies. Each £1 share cost 15s 6d, was free of income tax and could be redeemed five years later.

To draw attention to the schemes there were big events, like the Tank Bank, which came to Manchester on 18 December 1917. The Tank Bank was situated in Albert Square with an office in the Town Hall to take deposits from the general public. There was an expectation that the total amount collected would outdo Liverpool – which in its first three days had raised £797,800 – and Sheffield's £113,380, and with a degree of civic pride the *Manchester Guardian* reported that the city had hit £870,444 in just two days.[13]

The downside to this outpouring of money to the war effort was a squeeze on the existing charities. The Manchester and Salford Boys' and Girls' Refuges and Homes, set up in 1870, relied heavily on voluntary contributions and during the war experienced a huge reduction in what they received. It made regular appeals, highlighting the shortfall, and had to close four out of its five workshops with a loss of around £3,000 in earnings and proceeds from the work sold. Thankfully the charity did survive, changing its name to the Together Trust in 1920 and moving out of the city, and continues to work helping young people, vulnerable adults and families.

The war altered daily life in the city in many ways. Railway journeys became increasingly difficult as more of the network was given over to the needs of the military, and the cost of travel increased. Mr Fred B. Davis of Bankfield Avenue, who worked 30 miles from his home, complained bitterly in the *Manchester Guardian* at the cost of travelling to work. Before the war, he wrote, he could get a weekend ticket for 3*s* 6*d* but now the journey cost 7*s* 7*d*, leaving him to comment that this was rather a large sum to pay for the privilege of going home.[14]

At the end of 1916 the Railway Executive announced that, along with a further reduction in train services, the reservation of seats, compartments and saloons was to cease, with fewer sleeping and dining cars, and there would be luggage restrictions. It was a dismal message conceding that train journeys would be longer, slower, less frequent and would cost more. It was a policy designed to deter people from using the trains for pleasure and instead maintain a service sufficient for those who were compelled to travel for business or other reasons.[15]

During the following two years more services were cut. In March 1917 fifty-three trains between Manchester and Stockport, Buxton, Crewe and Warrington were axed, along with the closure of ten small stations outside the city, and, a year later, with the last big German offensive in full swing, twenty-six trains serving Manchester ceased running.

It was a state of affairs which, by the summer of 1918, had left many in Manchester contemplating a holiday at home. The August Bank Holiday had seen the railway stations fairly busy in the morning as some tried their luck at the seaside (Blackpool claimed record numbers of visitors), but there were fewer people coming into the city to spend the holiday compared with former years. For those Mancunians unable or unwilling to chance the trains, one newspaper reported that at least the city's parks provided the opportunity to spend long hours amid pleasant surroundings. All of which meant that the trams out to Heaton Park, Platt Fields and Didsbury were full and the attractions of Belle Vue Gardens, the theatres and picture houses were 'crowded to overflowing'.[16] But the weather proved indifferent and while there were the odd bouts of sunshine it remained overcast for most of the day.

Just seven months after the outbreak of war, the prime minister had been forced to explain why the price of wheat, sugar and coal had risen dramatically and set the blame on a mix of international reasons compounded by labour shortages and transport problems caused by the war. It was an argument which the Labour Party leader said failed to acknowledge the growing temptation by some to take advantage of the shortages and raise prices, and called for Parliament to intervene.[17] Nor was he alone in believing that some were profiteering at the expense of the general public. There was evidence supported by prosecutions that some were taking advantage of the disruption to food supplies.

This was compounded by the German U-boat campaign, which began to reduce the amount of food coming into the country. At the close of 1915 Britain had imported 30,000 tons of butter which, by December 1917, had fallen to under 3,000 tons. The official line at the beginning of 1917 was that there was no problem and even by March Mrs Peel of the Ministry of Food commented that while the food position was serious, there was every reason to hope that if people carried out the recommendations of Lord Davenport, the Minister of Food Control, the country would come through what she conceded was a very difficult period.[18]

The recommendations had included an appeal for families to adopt 'The National Scale of Voluntary Rations' of 4lb of bread or 3lb of flour, 2½lb of meat and ¾lb of sugar per week, which was the allowances already in place for people eating in restaurants and hotels.

All houses agreeing to do this received a small placard which proclaimed: IN HONOUR BOUND WE ADOPT THE

NATIONAL SCALE OF VOLUNTARY RATIONS. There is anecdotal evidence suggesting that it had some success, especially amongst the middle class, but it obscured the fact that shortages had been pushing the price of food up since the beginning of the war, causing increasing hardship amongst the poor and the working classes.

The Food Vigilance Committees, established by the Labour Movement at the outbreak of the war, continued to highlight the issues of food shortages and price rises and demanded that the production and distribution of food should be taken over by the government in partnership with the trade unions and Co-operative societies. The Committees had also argued for food rationing and even bolder moves to alleviate the problem, including the public supply and distribution of milk, meals for mothers and young children, and the establishment of municipal kitchens.

The government, however, remained opposed to compulsory rationing despite the growing evidence of shortages and its impact on the poor, with the Food Controller asserting in a speech at Manchester Town Hall in early November that this was

Manchester Corporation Tramways employees in 1915. Of the 3,000 who enlisted, 310 were killed.

the voluntary scheme's last chance.[19] And that proved to be the case, for later in the month the government gave in and began rationing. It started in the January and was confined to sugar but by April had been extended to include meat, butter, cheese and margarine.

In March, Manchester, unlike other cities, saw its tea ration reduced to an ounce per person, but a few months later looked forward to the abolition of 'meatless days' in its restaurants, while in the run-up to Christmas the meat rations were relaxed, allowing families to use all their meat coupons to buy chickens and turkeys.

NOTES

1 Preparing Voluntary Aid in Manchester, *Manchester Guardian*, 17 August 1914
2 The Red Cross in East Lancashire, *Manchester Guardian*, 27 November 1914
3 Mr George Bigwood, Correspondence, *Manchester Guardian*, 29 January 1915
4 Red Cross Orderlies, Mr F.F. Christopher, *Manchester Guardian*, 1 February 1915
5 Woodlawn, Didsbury, from East Lancashire Branch of the British Red Cross Society, Sherratt & Hughes, 1916, p. 84
6 Willow Bank, Moss Side, from East Lancashire Branch of the British Red Cross Society, p. 98
7 The Red Cross Work of East Lancashire Branch, *Manchester Guardian*, 3 May 1915
8 British Red Cross Christmas at Woodlawn, *Manchester Guardian*, 30 December 1916
9 Sales by Auction, *Manchester Guardian*, 14 May 1919
10 Colman, A.P., letter to the principal teacher, St Clements Infants' School, Chorlton, St Clements Parish Church Magazine, October 1917
11 Hansard House of Lords Debate, 18 April 1923, vol. 53 cc 714–24
12 Advert for 'Fag Day', *Daily Mirror*, 7 June 1916
13 The Tanks Second Try, Manchester Climbing to the Top, *Manchester Guardian*, 19 December 1917
14 The New Railway Fares, *Manchester Guardian*, 30 January 1917
15 New Railway Service, *Manchester Guardian*, 28 December 1916
16 Manchester and Train Rationing, *Manchester Guardian*, 6 August 1918

4

LIFE ON THE HOME FRONT

It was clear from very early on that the large numbers of men volunteering would impact on the labour market, offering up new opportunities for women in a range of occupations. This was a situation which was made more pressing with the introduction of conscription in 1916.

At the beginning it manifested itself with a surge of voluntary offers for everything from nurses to dispatch riders and interpreters to help with Belgian refugees. The Women's War Emergency Corps reported that in the first three weeks of August there were between 5,000 and 6,000 'of the most efficient women anxious to serve in the most effective way'[1] on their register. This surge of voluntary support extended to offering up homes as hospitals and hospitality to working girls in the holidays or during unemployment. The papers regularly advertised the names and addresses of women engaged in charitable work, particularly those running the 'comforts sections'.

But as important as this charitable work was, the growing demand for women to replace men in the workplace took on a pace during 1915. In May of that year Salford Corporation took on fifteen women to work as guards on their trams and a few months later Manchester followed suit, while the Manchester postal authorities decided to utilise the services of women in the 'delivery of letters'. This followed an appeal by the Board

Magnesia and gripe water ... looking after baby, 1916.

of Trade in March for women to register for work at their local Labour Exchange, and in the course of the next three years women were to be found working in heavy industry, as well as on the land, in offices and on the transport network.

Of course in many respects none of this was new. For over a century women had worked in textile mills and coal mines, laboured alongside men in the fields and done a variety of dirty and unpleasant occupations often for little remuneration. But the scope of their involvement and the fact that many of these occupations were new to women marked a sea change, as did the fact that some of these occupations were far better paid than their previous jobs.

MISS REBECCA CHAPMAN

Miss Rebecca Chapman was appointed as 'Driver conductor' for the Salford Corporation Tramways in 1918 and was sufficiently proud of her job that she retained both the handbook issued to 'Female Conductors' along with her licence and certificate of employment.

She was 18 years old when she was appointed in August 1918 and her handbook records that her conductor's uniform number was 98, and that she lived at Worthington Lodge, Park Lane in Higher Broughton.

The handbook lists a fascinating set of instructions running to 49 pages and covering everything from pay to the collection of fares, safety and the maintenance of the tram car. She was expected to be 'firm, civil and obliging in the execution of her duty at all times' and was forbidden from accepting any form of gratuity.

The job was not without a few dangers. Just a week after she had started Rebecca recorded in the back of the handbook that she had 'fallen off' the tram at 11.40 on Thursday 17 September.

Worthington Lodge was a large house with twenty-one rooms and twelve cellars and in stark contrast to the two-roomed house on Hodson Street which she had shared with her widowed mother and six siblings in Salford in 1911. All of which may mean that her job on the Salford Trams was a significant new occupation. Not that her appointment was without opposition. Tram workers in Salford had argued that 'the work of a guard is not a woman's work and that it would be too much to expect that women should take charge of the early workmen's cars or the late cars which would keep them up until midnight.'

Two munitions girls.

By the end of 1914 plans were in place to employ 10-15,000 women in munitions factories, but by June 1915 the number enrolled for munitions work actually stood at 78,946. In Manchester many were employed in factories and workshops converted from other uses.

Their entry into the labour movement was not met with universal approval. They faced opposition from work colleagues and those in charge. Some of the concerns centred around the fear that employing women might drive down wages, while those in positions of responsibility sometimes made cheap comments. In 1918 Mr Frederick A. Price, the Superintendent of the Manchester Gas Department, reporting to the Gas Committee of Manchester Corporation on the work of the thirty-one women clerks and eighty-five women meter inspectors, concluded that while they were good and careful workers, industrious and painstaking, they lacked initiative, were not capable of discharging the higher administrative duties, and lacked the necessary imagination and concentration with the power of organisation, adding they liked to indulge in a little gossip.[2]

Not quite equality yet for Miss Chapman on her Salford Tram. 'D'ye Ken I dinna believe in women having this job!'

D'ye ken, I dinna believe in women having this job !

In May 1915 Mrs Annot Robinson, who had long campaigned for improved working conditions and the extension of the vote to women, pointed out that:

women will most certainly have to take the place of men. There is already a shortage of men workers in Manchester but so far as I am aware no woman taking on a man's work will be receiving a man's wage. Women have already been employed in the printing trade and the hardware industry, but are paid at much lower rates than the men for the same work.[3]

Miss Rebecca Chapman 'has permission to act as Driver Conductor', 9 September 1918.

Miss Rebecca Chapman was granted a licence as a 'conductoress on any Tramway Carriage from 9 September 1918 till 30 June 1919'.

'Fares please!' – a clippie.

It was a state of affairs that led to the establishment of the Women's Interests Committee in May 1915, 'with a view to investigating and making public the conditions of women employed in munitions factories.'[4] At its first conference it called for a guaranteed minimum wage of £1 per week for 48 hours for women in the munitions industry, with piecework rates set at a minimum of £1 per week, overtime pay at a time and a quarter, improved conditions for night work, and the provision of canteens.

In March 1916, according to the Secretary of the Women's Interests Committee, the average weekly wage in Manchester for an adult woman working on munitions was less than 14s, a third of what a man was paid.[5] And the work could be both heavy and dangerous, especially in the munitions factories. There was the ever-present threat of explosions along with the effect of exposure to chemicals in the cordite and TNT, which in some cases caused the skin to turn yellow occasioning the nickname 'canaries', which was used along with the more affectionate 'munitionettes'.

Comic comments on munitions work.

That's the stuff to give 'em!

WHAT'S THAT! YOU'VE GOT THE SACK AT THE MUNITION WORKS! — WHAT FOR?

I DUNNO — I NEVER DONE NOTHING

In response to the rising cost of living the Labour Movement set up Local Emergency War Committees and Food Vigilance Committees, which reported to the War Emergency Workers National Committee in London. The idea of Food Vigilance Committees seems oddly old-fashioned, but back in 1915 it was seen by many as an essential way of preventing the growing practice of adulterating food and the rise in the cost of living. They were joint bodies made up of representatives from co-operative societies, local trades councils, the Labour Party and other organisations. They set out clear policies on how to manage shortages by insisting that:

> the Government purchase all essential imported food stuffs, commandeer or control all home grown food products and make effective use of ships and the control of transport facilities, thereby securing both a fair share of what was available and at a controlled price.[6]

A key part of this would be the local authorities' power 'to deal with the distribution of food stuffs and coal, and to establish Municipal Kitchens'.

The Food Vigilance Committees also reported to the National Committee in London and, along with Local Emergency War Committees, the reports provide a vivid picture of the effect of the war. In 1915 the Stockport Labour Party commented on the level of representation on pensions committees, and Mr J. Robinson of the Stockport branch of the Tailors Society queried the rates for making khaki tunics. Later, in 1917, the National Committee was engaged in the registration of shops in Manchester and the rising price of coal.

In February 1915 the Labour Movement staged a major public meeting to highlight the issue of rising prices and demanded government intervention. It was co-ordinated by the Manchester and Salford Trades Council in conjunction with the Gorton Trades Council, the Labour Party and Independent Labour Party, and other smaller socialist groups

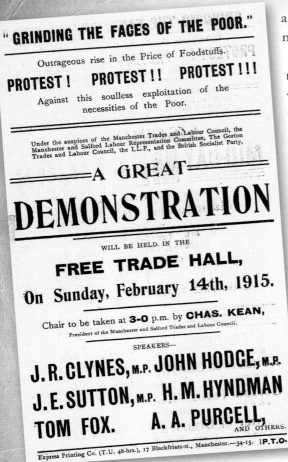

"GRINDING THE FACES OF THE POOR."

Outrageous rise in the Price of Foodstuffs.

PROTEST! PROTEST!! PROTEST!!!

Against this soulless exploitation of the necessities of the Poor.

Under the auspices of the Manchester Trades and Labour Council, the Manchester and Salford Labour Representation Committee, The Gorton Trades and Labour Council, the I.L.P., and the British Socialist Party,

=A GREAT=

DEMONSTRATION

WILL BE HELD IN THE

FREE TRADE HALL,

On Sunday, February 14th, 1915.

Chair to be taken at **3-0** p.m. by **CHAS. KEAN,**

President of the Manchester and Salford Trades and Labour Council.

SPEAKERS—

J. R. CLYNES, M.P. JOHN HODGE, M.P.

J. E. SUTTON, M.P. H. M. HYNDMAN

TOM FOX. A. A. PURCELL,

AND OTHERS.

Express Printing Co. (T.U. 48-hrs.), 17 Blackfriars-st., Manchester.—34-15. [P.T.O.

Leaflet for the public meeting at the Free Trade Hall on 14 February 1915.

and was preceded by factory gate meetings across the city.

But the cost of living continued to rise, fuelling industrial unrest which continued throughout the war. The Munitions Acts of 1915 and 1916 had made strikes over pay and conditions illegal and instead substituted arbitration through tribunals. In theory this only applied to the manufacture of munitions but the tribunals consistently widened the scope of what was meant by munitions so that practically anything could be included, from the repair of a coal wagon to the supply of gas and the manufacture of bricks used to make homes for munitions workers.

Those who were found guilty could be fined or imprisoned with hard labour, but this failed to stop workers going on strike. In 1915 the dock workers at the Port of Manchester, along with railwaymen and engineers, came out on strike and were followed later in the war by cotton workers, carters and tram workers. By 1917, as the number of strikes rose, the government established a Commission of Inquiry into the industrial unrest in the North West. Its opening sessions were held in Manchester and later moved to Liverpool before returning to the city. It drew on the evidence of employers, trade unions and the Labour Party and issued its report in the August of 1917, concluding that the grievances of the workers could be ranged under four headings: food prices, lack of confidence in government promises as to future conditions, the conduct of the medical boards, and liquor restrictions.[7] Added to this were grievances related to the regulations prohibiting workers leaving without the consent of their employer, issues over equality, and trade union recognition.

In Openshaw there was a dispute between the firm Armstrong Whitworth and the workforce over the dismissal of 121 men from the armour plate department without the relevant certificates allowing them to get work elsewhere. Just outside the city, in Oldham, the employees of the Co-op were in dispute over the Society's refusal to pay women the same rate as men, and at Sandbach the issue was the refusal of Foden's truck builders to recognise a trade union.

The war also threw up a raft of social problems, of which the rise in juvenile crime was one that exercised the concerns of pretty much everyone, from magistrates and teachers all the way up to the Home Secretary, and drew into the debate Sir Robert Baden-Powell, and an assortment of clergymen and 'experts'. No one doubted that there was a problem. At the Manchester City Sessions in July 1916, Mr A.J. Ashton, the Recorder, commented that of the seventeen prisoners before him nine were under age and eight were less than 18 years of age.[8] And later in the year Mr Spurley Hey, Manchester's Director of Education, in a report on juvenile crime in the city pointed out that the greatest tendency to commit offences was at 12 years of age.[9]

Not that there was any disagreement on the reasons why this was the case. The 'obvious' answer was due to the lack of parental control at a time when many fathers were away at the Front and mothers were working. This was seized upon by a succession of observers including the Bishop of Liverpool, who felt that owing to the war boys had been deprived of the corrective hand of the father while mothers did not seem to have the same authority over the children.

Equally likely to be cited was the impact of the cinema, which, according to one correspondent to the *Daily Telegraph*, was full of shows which focused on death, crime and killing, demoralising to both children and adults.

The report by Mr Hey also highlighted the fact that the majority of those involved in juvenile crime came from central Manchester, in what he described as the 'denser districts', making a telling point about the link between poverty and poor housing and pointing at the role of education in combating the problem. All of which was well and good but this was at a time when expenditure on education was being cut, trained teachers were leaving the profession for the Forces, and the increasing practice of a half-time system for some children whose schools had been taken over for military hospitals.

The recommendation of the government's Retrenchment Committee was to make savings of £200,000 with cuts to medical inspections, teacher training and technical school grants. Across the country local authorities were engaged in their own cost reductions. In Manchester the Education Committee had reduced its expenditure on higher education by £11,106 and on elementary education by £13,039, while Cheshire had reduced the leaving age for boys and girls from 14 to 13. This resulted in a degree of *ad hoc* provision for some pupils at least. In February 1916 the Manchester Museum reported that it was providing effective instruction for 900 to 1,000 children per week, drawn from the higher echelons of the elementary schools.[10] A similar scheme was underway at the City Art Gallery, the Whitworth Institute, and 'kindred institutes in the city', and had proved so popular that children not only travelled some distance to attend but even brought their parents.

By 1915 the number of schools taken over for military hospitals in Manchester amounted to eight. The first was the Central High School for Boys and Girls on Whitworth Street, which had 1,000 students and became the headquarters of the 2nd Western General Hospital. The following year another seven schools were taken over. These were Alfred Street in Harpurhey, Alma Park in Levenshulme, Grange Street in Bradford, Lilly Lane in Moston, Ducie Avenue, Moseley Road and Heald Place, which amounted to the loss of 3,897 school places.[11]

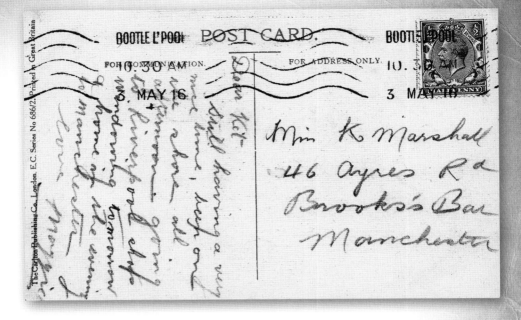

'Still having a nice time': Maggie's message to Kit on Ayres Road in Brook's Bar, 3 May 1916.

Amidst the dreary round of blackouts, rising prices and the ever lengthening casualty lists, there were those looking to the future and arguing that the war presented lessons for how Britain should be once peace returned. The Food Vigilance Committees had long been arguing for the involvement of the Labour and Co-operative Movement with the government in controlling the distribution and pricing of foodstuffs, and as early as 1915 there had been a recognition that after the war women should not be prevented from continuing in their wartime occupations. The theme behind much of this was that the sacrifice and the hardships endured should be met with a fairer society.

At a 1916 conference convened by the Manchester and District Women's Suffrage Societies and labour organisations the delegates argued for the involvement of the State in a whole range of social care issues, including the care of pre-school children and expectant mothers. It was, as Margret Ashton argued, an important question, particularly because many of the women 'being called out were married women and the State ought therefore to make provision for the proper care of their children'.[12] It followed then that the State should provide 'for the care of infant life in the form of schools for mothers … day nurseries and free nursery schools for children under school age' and that the control of these institutions should rest with boards appointed by local councils 'of which at least 50 per cent should be women of whom a fair proportion should be parents of the children'. A year later, a week-long campaign was launched in the city aimed at rousing 'a universal determination to prevent the unnecessary wastage of infant life, [focusing on] all the causes which make for the high rate of infant mortality.'[13]

But amid these visions for the future there remained a peace campaign rooted in the present. Opposition to the war never went away, picking up a degree of momentum as the causality lists grew ever longer and war weariness set in, and reaching a new pace with the introduction of conscription in 1916.

A key element of opposition to conscription came from women. Some, like Margaret Ashton and Mrs Annot Robinson, had been active in both the Labour Movement and the suffrage campaign before the war, and both were involved with the Women's International League (WIL) and the Women's Peace Crusade. The WIL had been founded in 1915 and was particularly strong in Manchester, where it had 573 members (which represented a quarter of the entire British membership).[14] The Women's Peace Crusade dated from the following year and flourished outside London.

The two women organised meetings and marches across the country, drawing large crowds. In Burnley Mrs Annot Robinson addressed a women-only meeting of between 4,000 and 5,000, while in nearby Nelson 1,200 attended a meeting in the local Methodist Sunday school, and across the Pennines in Leeds 3,000 turned up to hear the case against the war.

They were also active in smaller street-corner meetings, handing out leaflets in both Salford and Manchester highlighting casualty lists, and ran bigger meetings like the one in Stevenson Square in July 1917. This attracted a large audience who heard Margaret Ashton call for a negotiated peace with Germany, which went off with few interruptions. Elsewhere, meetings by the British Socialist Party were disrupted and broken up by hostile crowds.

Women were also active in the campaign to prevent conscription and after this had become law appeared as observers at the appeal tribunals for those men objecting to being conscripted.

There was no single type of conscientious objector. They were drawn from all classes and occupations and reflected opposition based on religious and moral grounds to political ones. Some were prepared to accept alternative 'service' while others maintained a total opposition to any activity which could remotely be seen as part of the war.

Harold Wild,
conscientious objector.

One study suggests that there were in excess of 200 conscientious objectors in Manchester, many of whom were members of the No Conscription Fellowship (NCF).[15] The NCF was established in the early months of the war by men who were not prepared to fight. Its Statement of Faith, adopted in 1915, recorded that it was an organisation of 'men likely to bear arms, who will refuse from conscientious motives to bear arms because they consider human life to be sacred.'[16]

After the passing of the Conscription Act the following year, part of the NFC's work revolved around helping those young men who were called in front of the tribunals to make their case for being exempted. There are many detailed accounts of tribunal hearings, ranging from press reports to the memoirs of those who appeared before the court.

Writing in 1920, John Graham, whose book remains a good history of the NFC, wrote that 'there was little uniformity in the practice of the Tribunals. The Local Tribunal in Liverpool was hopelessly tyrannical, the one in Manchester was judicial and reasonable.'[17]

In response to a prepared statement outlining the objector's opposition on religious or humanitarian grounds, questioning often revolved around what the objector would do if faced with a German invasion or, worse still, an attack on his own family. In many cases the members of the tribunals were both abrupt and unsympathetic to arguments of principle and quite scathing and dismissive in their comments. In response to the arguments of one objector, the Chairman of the Manchester Appeals Tribunal commented, 'it is [about] doing your duty. It is your duty to take part in the defence of your country and the public law of Europe.'

But not all the appeals were from conscientious objectors. Employers also appeared on behalf of employees who they judged were essential to their business. Along with these were individuals making out a personal case. In late March 1916 one Appeals Tribunal held in Manchester Town Hall heard from an editor of a local weekly newspaper, a man engaged in the textile advertising business, a shipping clerk and a variety troupe, who argued that the male member of the group was 'essential to a sketch [which] was their only means of a livelihood'.[18] Other appeals on the same day were on domestic grounds. The judgements varied from outright refusal to deferment for a short period. Our editor and the shipping clerk were granted a deferment for a month and the variety troupe were given two months.

But few of the thirty domestic appeals heard on the same day were accepted and in one case 'where four brothers were serving the country, exemption was only granted for two months to the fifth son of a widowed mother, the Chairman remarking that the woman was entitled to some consideration.'

'To May with best love from Frank …', Christmas card sent from the Sergeants' Mess, 23rd Service Battalion, Manchester Regiment.

One young man who could have exempted himself on medical grounds was Harold Wild, who was disabled and would have been judged unfit for military service, but because he was a pacifist chose instead to refuse to fight.

Born in 1896, Wild was a member of the Rusholme Wesleyan Methodist Church, and at one point considered ordination to

To May; with best love from Frank.

WITH EVERY GOOD WISH
FOR CHRISTMAS AND
THE NEW YEAR.

FROM

SERGEANTS' MESS,
23rd Service Battalion Manchester Regiment,
British Expeditionary Force,
1916 — 1917.

the Church. His response, when his call-up papers came, was to ignore them, which led to his arrest and a series of tribunal appearances. In a 1974 letter written to his daughter, he reflected that:

> looking back over the years, I do not feel that I could have taken any other stand than I did, involving one night in the Town Hall's Police cells, a ride in the 'Black Maria' to Minshull Street Police Station and a night in the 'Guard-room' of Ashton Barracks, followed by an interview before the Officer in charge (without any clothing on me). He was probably of the opinion that if I had tamely submitted myself to a normal military exam, I would have been rejected & he wanted to know WHY I refused military service.[19]

Throughout the period he kept a diary which explains the reasons behind his opposition to the war and paints a detailed picture of the peace campaign locally.[20] Writing in his diary on the evening of 31 December 1915 he concluded that, 'my life perhaps will be spent in fighting the Christian fight against Militarism in England.' And it was a fight spent at the sharp end of campaigning, including street meetings, the distribution of leaflets, as well as attending lectures and rallies, some of which were attended by the likes of Philip Snowden and Bertrand Russell. The meetings could range from a gathering at the gates of Alexandra Park to big set events in Milton Hall on Deansgate or the often rowdy events in Stevenson Square.

Chief amongst these were meetings of the NCF (of which he was an active member), meetings of the Independent Labour Party and British Socialist Party, along with those of various Christian groups.

Some days he packed two or three meetings in, travelling across the city and into the neighbouring townships. From March 1915 through to November 1918 he recorded a total of 147 meetings and lectures. They rose from twenty-one in 1915 to

Wound Badge belonging to Private Douglas Brown.

eighty-four during 1916, falling to eighteen in 1917 and twenty-four the following year.

Some of these meetings were attendant with danger from hostile crowds or police raids. On more than one occasion he wrote that a police raid was followed by arrests and the confiscation of peace literature. In June 1916 and again the following year he was 'detained and searched' following a police raid and casually reported on another occasion that 'on my way home I found a military raid in progress on the premises of Lyons Cafe, Market Street'.

Along the way he also attended tribunal meetings as an observer, visited a friend in prison for refusing to serve, and comforted the mother of another friend killed in action. But he also spent time rambling in the countryside, visiting the theatre and variety halls as well as the cinema, but even here the war was never far away. At the end of October 1916 he recorded that he had been to the 'Queens Picture Palace, Longsight where I saw 'The Battle of the Somme' film. How after seeing such a picture anyone can desire victory before peace amazes me.'

The film had been premiered in London on 10 August and went on general release on 21 August and was seen by around 20 million people in Britain during the first six weeks. Opinions ranged from those who found the film disturbing and in bad taste to those like Mr Robert Heatley, writing to the *Manchester Guardian* from his Chambers in Brazenose Street, who felt that 'anything that gives us an insight into the horrors and discomforts our troops are suffering must awaken a sense of admiration for their bravery, and inspire us with a desire to do all we can for them whilst on the field of battle and on their return home.'[21]

NOTES

1   The Women's Emergency Corps, *Manchester Guardian*, 27 August 1914
2   Women at Men's Work, *Manchester Guardian*, 5 January 1918
3   *Daily Citizen*, 20 March 1915
4   Women's War Interests, Work of the Manchester and District Committee, The Common Cause, 3 March 1916
5   Correspondence, *Manchester Guardian*, 21 January 1916
6   The London Food Vigilance Committee, 1915
7   Industrial Unrest, Commissioner's Report on Lancashire, *Manchester Guardian*, 1 August 1917
8   Increase in Juvenile Crime, *Manchester Guardian*, 27 July 1916
9   Juvenile Crime, *Manchester Guardian*, 28 October 1916
10 War Service in the Museums, Teaching the Half Timers, *Manchester Guardian*, 21 February 1916
11 2nd Western General Hospital, Manchester, 1914–1919, Margaret Elwin Sparshot
12 State and the Mother's Duty, *Manchester Guardian*, 9 May 1916
13 Baby Week, Opening of the Campaign in Manchester, *Manchester Guardian*, July 1917
14 Liddlington, Jill, *The Long Road to Greenham*, 1989, Virago Press Ltd, p. 119
15 Pearce, Cyril, Typical Conscientious Objectors – A Better Class of Conscience? No-Conscription Fellowship Image Management and the Manchester Contribution, Manchester Regional History Review, 2004, p. 44
16 Graham, John W., *Conscription and Conscience, A History 1916–1919*, 1922, George Allen & Unwin Ltd
17 Ibid., p. 69
18 Mind of the Conscientious Objector, *Manchester Guardian*, 30 March 1916
19 Letter from Harold Wild to Dorothy Spence (*née* Wild), 17 November 1974
20 Wild, Harold, The Diary of a Conscientious Objector, 1915–1919, Dorothy Spence (ed.), published online: www.olioweb.me.uk/echoes/?page_id=232
21 The Battle of the Somme Film, *Manchester Guardian*, 2 September 1916

5

ARMISTICE

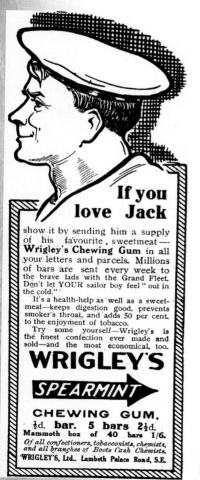

The date of the end of the Great War is fixed for most of us by the phrase, 'at the eleventh hour of the eleventh month' and sits with that equally much-quoted comment by Sir Edward Grey four years earlier that 'The lamps are going out all over Europe'.[1] Together they are the two markers between which fall the story of that conflict, which is often then divided neatly into distinctive and easy history.

The year 1914 was that short period when the country willingly and enthusiastically embraced the war, 1915 the year of adjustment, while the following two were dominated by the awful losses on the Western Front and the transformation of the country as it mobilized for total war. Which leaves 1918 as the year the war ended (in fact it rumbled on into November and those eleven months were ones of continued strikes, food shortages, the start of the flu epidemic and some disastrous military events). Added to which were further restrictions on the opening times of cinemas, theatres and restaurants, and in April plans were put in place to ration coal. The loss of 50,000 miners to the military and the increased demand from munitions works meant that householders could expect to see cuts of 25-30 per cent. There had been a mild winter and many of those who had taken the government's advice and stockpiled coal were in a good position, but these were always the better off who could afford to buy in bulk and had the cellars to accommodate the supplies.

Early in April the expectation from the Board of Trade was that householders with one or two rooms would be allowed 2 tons and 10cwt for the year, rising to 21 tons for those with twelve rooms (a large bag of coal

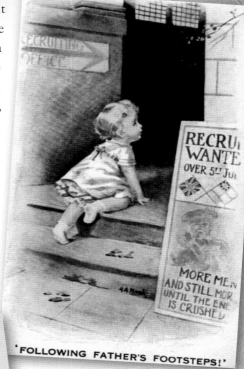

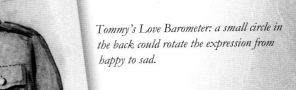

'FOLLOWING FATHER'S FOOTSTEPS!'

Following in Father's footsteps.

Tommy's Love Barometer: a small circle in the back could rotate the expression from happy to sad.

Opposite: Chewing the Wrigley Way, 1916.

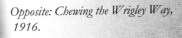

weighed 1cwt which is 50kg and there are 20cwt or twenty bags to a ton). To a modern reader this may still seem a large amount but given that for many families that coal would not only heat the home but provide fuel to both heat water and cook with, fifty bags for a year was not much.

As if that were not enough, the news from the Western Front was appalling. In March the Germans launched their last major offensive of the war and in the thick of that campaign were the 1st and 2nd City Battalions.

During February, the 1st City Battalion was defending a position known as Manchester Hill and in the face of a German attack in late March held on bravely till they were overwhelmed. On the first day they lost eighty men and in the course of the nine days of fighting the battalion were reduced from twenty-three officers and 717 men to just one officer and 116 men.[2] The 2nd City Battalion also sustained heavy casualties and in the immediate aftermath the two were formed into a composite battalion which suffered further heavy losses. So appalling were these losses that both were temporally reassigned as training units and later in June the 2nd was disbanded and the 1st returned to Britain.

Reflecting on the events at the April meeting of the Council, the Lord Mayor paid tribute 'to the bravery of the Manchester soldiers who made so firm a stand in the recent fighting' and later in the month a memorial service was held in the cathedral.

Back on the Western Front the German offensive which caused such heavy losses to the 1st and 2nd City Battalions could not be maintained and the Allied counter-offensive in August pushed the Germans back. By early September each of the Central Powers was seeking peace terms. Bulgaria was first to sign an Armistice on 29 September, the Ottoman Empire followed a month later, by which time the Austro-Hungarian Empire was falling apart. In Germany, as early as the beginning of August it was clear that a military victory was no longer possible and with the threat of social disruption

The Manchester Regiment lost 13,000 men, of these 4,700 were from the Manchester Pals Battalions. The Lancashire Fusiliers, which also recruited from Manchester and Salford, lost 13,600 men.

events moved quickly. The Kaiser's abdication on 9 November was followed by the proclamation of a German republic.

On the same day the *Manchester Guardian* confidently asserted that 'The world-war is over' but railed against the slowness of the new German Government to accept the Allied peace terms. But it was a mere glitch and by ten o'clock on the morning of 11 November news that the Armistice had been concluded spread across the city, aided by the sound of sirens.

MOTHER, WHY DOESN'T DADDY COME HOME?

'Mother, Why Doesn't Daddy Come Home?'

*Armistice Day
outside the Palace
Theatre of Varieties,
Oxford Street.*

Just before 11 a.m., as the war was ending, the crowd in Albert Square fell silent as two flags were raised at the Town Hall, and with that 'the full day of jubilation came up fast. The frequency of blue linen overalls in the streets announced that the munitions workers had broken loose and by one o'clock the streets had formalized themselves into processions which gathered as a snowball gathers bulk.'[3] By the afternoon 'on all the main roads in the city, along Ashton Old Road, along Stockport Road and Hyde Road, work girls poured in hundreds gathering as they went flags and other patriotic symbols.'

Many of the city's shops were closed by midday, the tram service gradually slackened with women guards and trolley girls abandoning their posts, and by early evening the tramway system was practically at a standstill. And with darkness came the end of the blackout, although the Home Office was quick to point out that while the masking of street lamps might be removed, the coal shortages would restrict the number of street lamps that could be lit. Not that this stopped the celebrations. People began to come in from the outlying Lancashire towns aided by the numbers of employers of mills and workshops who agreed to pay wages for two days' holidays. The streets became so crowded that traffic was almost ground to a halt. Many of the processions were headed up by bands and, in the words of one journalist, 'crowds that moved as if they had no care and no thought beyond the burning joy of the moment.'

Like all such events the solemn rubbed shoulders with the irreverent, so while some poured in to a special thanksgiving service at the cathedral, across the city at the Palace Theatre a crowd of between 500 and 600 people gate-crashed a matinee performance without paying. The manager told the leaders he 'should not attempt to stop them and that he supposed they would pay him some time'. The solitary policeman on the door was overwhelmed and carried up into the circle, while the performance was so disrupted by the singing and cheering of the crowd that a fifteen-minute interval was arranged with the orchestra playing patriotic songs and the manager quoting from the prime minister's speech.

It was a pattern of behaviour imitated in music halls across the city and one that was replicated the following day, with more crowds partying on the streets. The munitions factories all closed on that second day with some big firms staying shut till 14 November. At least some of those munitions workers 'swarmed into the entrance-hall of the Town Hall where the clogs clattered merrily upon the tessellated pavement'.

Peace picture postcard, 1919.

By contrast the young conscientious objector Harold Wild passed the evening of 9 November 'writing envelopes to assist R.J. Davis the Labour candidate in West Salford' and reflected in his diary a few days later that, 'I find it absolutely extraordinary that my father never mentioned the signing of the Armistice on 11 November 1918!'[4]

The following month would see a succession of memorial services for those who had died fighting. Earlier in the year there had been services to remember the men who had perished in the Gallipoli campaign of 1915, those from the Somme the following year, and for the members of the University and Public Schools Battalion which had been founded in September 1914 from 'members of the northern universities and young men of public school and university training in the great places of business in Manchester'.

But of all the ceremonies, the event in the Town Hall on 21 December struck one of the most powerful notes. On that day the 8th (Ardwick) Battalion of the Manchester Regiment received back 'the colours that they had placed in the Town Hall for safekeeping when it went away on active service'. The battalion, the Lord Mayor said, 'belonged to the Territorial's, and 98 per cent of the men offered themselves for service. They served in Egypt, then in Cyprus and on 4 June 1915 they had a severe experience of war. Out of twenty-two officers who went into action with them only two returned.'[5]

Against the jubilation at the end of the war was another threat – an influenza epidemic. It had begun in the summer, returned later in the autumn, and impacted on industry and commerce, briefly disrupting the tram service and leading to the closure of all Manchester schools on 30 November.[6] And, despite the medical authorities concluding that the outbreak was 'reaching the culminating point' and anticipating a decline from the start of December, they called for the closure of all Sunday schools and recommended that children under 14 should be barred from cinemas and theatres – a wise precaution given that the death toll had risen through November from eighty-one at the end of the first week to 297 by 23 November, which is shocking enough but is more so when expressed as a percentage of total deaths. At the beginning of the month deaths from flu had amounted to 32 per cent of all recorded deaths but by the fourth week that figure had climbed to 53 per cent.

Flu deaths during November 1918	
Week ending	No. of deaths
2 November	81
9 November	14
16 November	220
23 November	297

According to one newspaper the mortuaries were full, undertakers couldn't keep pace with the orders, and at the cemeteries the labour available for grave digging had proved quite inadequate. This led to efforts to release skilled coffin makers from the army and a call for 'greater simplicity in funeral arrangements and a more extensive use of the crematorium'.

As ever there were those who were swift to make money from the crisis: the firm Genatosan Ltd offered up their 'Germ Killing Throat Tablet', Formamint, which would ensure 'you will be safe from Spanish Influenza and other epidemics'. It was endorsed by Lady Manns, Lady Jane Joicey-Cecil and Mr Matheson Lang, who was ordered by his doctor to take Formamint, which 'gave me great relief'.[7] But perhaps we shouldn't be over harsh on the makers of Formamint for offering their tablet as a remedy given that at least some thought that there might a link between the outbreak and the arrival of American troops, who landed shortly before the epidemic began.

A real positive in the year was the extension of the parliamentary vote to virtually all men and eight million or so women. The bitter struggles of the immediate post-war period and the massive contribution women made had, it seemed, been vindicated. Margaret Ashton, who had long campaigned for women's suffrage, remarked at a reception to celebrate the event 'that a great victory had been won ... Women had at last that weapon in their hands which would bring real victory.' But she also went on to point out that 'it was only the beginning' and of course that was the case. The 1918 Act extended the vote to women over the age of 30 who were householders, the wives of householders, occupiers of property with an annual rent of £5, and graduates of British universities. It would be another ten years before all women over the age of 21 were eligible to vote. Looking ahead to that moment, Margaret Ashton concluded that only then 'should we be able to talk of democracy for the first time in this country [with] women taking their share in politics.'[8]

As ever the devil was in the detail, as fellow campaigner Mrs Annot Robinson pointed out at one of the meetings held to listen to appeals by women who wished to be on the electoral list. There was, she pointed out, a clear problem for women who were over 30 but living at home with their parents. If they couldn't prove they paid rent for an unfurnished room within the family home they were not eligible to be on the register. In the case of two sisters from Withington who lived with their mother, 'both furnished their bedrooms and were both in business [but] they paid no rent – instead each paid 30s per week for "their keep".'

Mrs Annot Robinson

Born in Scotland in 1874, Annot Robinson was a well known and respected campaigner for women's rights during the early part of the twentieth century and, with the outbreak of war, worked to highlight the exploitation of women in the workplace, the scandal of war profiteering, and the need to explore a way to end the conflict.

She had become active in Scottish politics in the 1890s and by 1895 was working for the Independent Labour Party in Dundee.

Upon marriage she moved to Ancoats but when this ended in separation she continued her political work in Manchester as a single parent. She joined the Woman's Social and Political Union (WSPU), spoke at rallies in favour of votes for women and was imprisoned in 1908 and 1909. But like other socialists she eventually broke with the WSPU over what she saw as the dictatorial leadership of Mrs Pankhurst and the Union's support for the war. Instead Annot Robinson campaigned for a peaceful conclusion to the fighting, was an organiser of the Manchester branch of the Women's International League for Peace and Freedom, and was one of the first signatories to the open letter to the Women of Austria and Germany at the end of 1914 calling for peace. She also worked to improve the working conditions of women and highlighted the lack of equality in pay for women in a range of industries but particularly the new munitions factories. She was also an active member of the Independent Labour Party and stood for election on two municipal elections after the war.

Contemporary media reports reveal her speeches, letters to newspapers and private correspondence, such as a letter written to the *Manchester Guardian* on 17 October 1908 and occasioned by the 'distress amongst the unemployed women of Manchester [which] is so acute this week and the administration of relief so slow, that I feel impelled to draw attention to the condition of affairs', and in particular to a young woman she had seen faint in Parsonage Gardens 'for want of food'.

Annot Robinson returned to Scotland in 1923, where she died two years later.

"GRINDING THE FACES OF THE POOR."

Outrageous rise in the Price of Foodstuffs.

PROTEST ! PROTEST !! PROTEST !!!

Against this soulless exploitation of the necessities of the Poor.

Under the auspices of the Manchester Trades and Labour Council, the Manchester and Salford Labour Representation Committee, The Gorton Trades and Labour Council, the I.L.P., and the British Socialist Party,

A GREAT

DEMONSTRATION

WILL BE HELD IN THE

FREE TRADE HALL,

On Sunday, February 14th, 1915.

Chair to be taken at **3-0** p.m. by **CHAS. KEAN,**
President of the Manchester and Salford Trades and Labour Council.

SPEAKERS—

J. R. CLYNES, M.P. JOHN HODGE, M.P.

J. E. SUTTON, M.P. H. M. HYNDMAN

TOM FOX. A. A. PURCELL,

AND OTHERS.

Express Printing Co. (T.U. 48-hrs.), 17 Blackfriars-st., Manchester.—34·15. [P.T.O.

'Outrageous rise in the price of foodstuffs': a leaflet advertising a public meeting at the Free Trade Hall on 14 February 1915, which was attended by Mrs Annot Robinson.

Upon such fine detail turned their chance to vote and while the Deputy Returning Officer judged that part of that 30s was for the upkeep of the house and this qualified them as tenants, in other parts of the country an alternative interpretation was placed on what constituted rent.

A more pressing consideration for many in the days and weeks after the war finished was the very real prospect that they would become unemployed. Manchester was one of the largest centres for engineering and many factories had been completely turned over to making shells. It was assumed that as government contracts ceased large numbers of workers would be dismissed and there was no doubting that the impact would be primarily on women. One local firm before the war had employed very few women but by 1918 counted 3,000 on the payroll.

And for those with men and women serving abroad, there was now an anxious wait for their return. By 27 December 5,931 officers, 105,717 other ranks and 4,235 civilians had been repatriated. Of these 623 were Allied prisoners of war, men like Private Albert Derry, who was 25 years old when he was captured during the last big German offensive on the Western Front in March 1918.

It was the first day of that big attack and it is easy to understand the anxiety his family must have gone through, knowing that his battalion, the Lancashire Fusiliers, were in the thick of the fighting. It would not be until May that they got confirmation

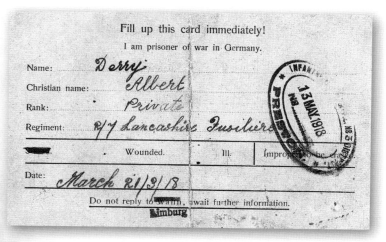

'I am a prisoner of war in Germany': a POW card from Albert Derry of the Lancashire Fusiliers, March 1918.

that he was a prisoner of war at Limburg an der Lahn. The camp held 12,000 British soldiers, who remained in captivity till the end of the war.

Private Derry had been born in 1893, one of eight children. His father, a shoe repairer, had married Frances in 1880 and by 1911 they were living at 155 Church Road in Pendleton. In May 1918 Limburg an der Lahn must have seemed a long way from the butcher's shop Albert had worked in before the war. His army records were lost in the Blitz and while we know that he was awarded the British War Medal and the Allied Victory Medal, what happened to him on his return has yet to be discovered.

But even as the men and women were coming home many more would still be away from Britain as Christmas approached. 'With peace in the air,' the *Manchester Guardian* reported, 'whatever happens in the next few weeks, 74 battalions of Lancashire and Cheshire men will stand at their posts.'[9] And that occasioned a fourth *Manchester Guardian* appeal for comforts for the troops, for 'no army has ever been so scattered before – in the new won departments of France and Belgium, in Italy, in the Balkan hills, in India, in Baluchistan, in Syria and Mesopotamia, even on the northern plains of Russia.' Gifts could be in money or kind and the newspaper was prepared to arrange for 200 cigarettes to be sent out carriage-free to men whose employers subscribed to the fund.

The scope and concern for the numbers of disabled servicemen grew with the course of the war. As early as November 1914 one delegate at a conference of Labour Socialist and Co-operative organisations held at Caxton Hall in Manchester pointed out that 'a man who was temporarily disabled was paid a pension of from 6d to 1s 6d a day until he was restored to health,' and asked 'how could a family live on that amount?'[10] But, despite the government's decision a few months later to establish a 'strong committee to look into the possibility of providing employment for disabled soldiers' and their recognition that the care of those disabled was a 'national obligation', it was, according to the MP Dr Macnamara, not 'so immediately pressing'.

By August 1918 the government was calling on employers of munitions factories to show a preference for discharged disabled servicemen, which echoed an appeal in June by the Manchester Chamber of Commerce for its members to provide suitable work for discharged and partially disabled soldiers. Added to this, a rolling set of exhibitions focusing on the job opportunities open to the disabled were planned, with the first in Manchester at the Free Trade Hall in the September.

Already in both Manchester and Salford work had been done through the War Pensions and Education Committee. Salford had specialized in training men for engineering, as well as boot- and shoe-making, while at Manchester in the Mill Street centre training had been on tailoring, boot and shoe repair, and watch repair. The training lasted for roughly twelve months. As early as March 1918 Salford Education Committee had reported that their training scheme had received 110 entries, of which fifty men had either left or been discharged; twenty had been placed

An unknown couple.

in employment and forty-five were continuing their training in the workshops.

The Salford War Pensions Committee had in June made an appeal for voluntary helpers who would be willing to join a Salford Discharged Friendly Aid Detachment and regularly visit some of the disabled men. The appeal pointed out that:

> several thousands have returned to Salford and the local Committee is faced with the growing and difficult problem of attending to their needs. Some of them are broken in health and spirit and they need the stimulus of sympathetic care of a friend who can help to secure for each soldier the appropriate right either of a pension, or gratuity, or medical treatment or training for a new occupation.[11]

A little later a Manchester orthopaedic hospital was planned for the Grangethorpe estate adjoining Platt Fields which, in addition to the hospital buildings, would be fitted with treatment rooms with electrical baths, a gymnasium and curative workshops.

But for those returning to civilian life, whether they had been injured or not, things were not always so simple. The National Federation of Discharged and Demobilised Sailors and Soldiers campaigned on behalf of those who had left the armed service, and in October 1918 won a by-election in Harpurhey. The Manchester branch of the Federation, which had 3,900 local members, argued that it should be represented on the City Council given that the Corporation employed such a large work-force. (It was already in dispute with several of the City Council's departments – including the Waterworks – over sick pay and with another department over the promise of reinstatement for men who had enlisted.)

The result of the election was a win for the Federation whose candidate, a Mr John Welan, secured almost 61 per cent of the total vote over his Labour opponent. The election was fought on the new register which had been compiled after the extension of the vote to women.

Advert for His Master's Voice, 1916.

HEAR ROBERT RADFORD

England's Greatest Bass

From a photo by Dover St. Studios.

ON 'HIS MASTER'S VOICE'

THE RECORDS OF PERFECT TONAL PURITY.

TO listen to Robert Radford singing on 'His Master's Voice' Records is to hear the finest bass voice in England, reproduced in its full richness and beauty. Every shade of tone and expression is caught and rendered with exact fidelity by these wonderful records.

ASK OUR DEALERS TO PLAY THESE RECORDS TO YOU.

10-inch Records, 3/6
4-2319. Drake goes West (*Sanderson*)
3-2798. D'ye ken John Peel (with chorus)
3-2894. Glorious Devon (*German*)
3-2934. Simon the Cellarer (*Hatton*)
12-inch Records, 5/6
02437. Blow, blow, thou winter wind (*Sarjeant*)

12-inch Records, 5/6
02616. The Windmill (*Nelson*)
02102. I'm a Roamer (*Mendelssohn*)
02451. The Palms (*Faure*) (and Westminster Cathedral Choir)
02085. The Village Blacksmith (*Weiss*) (with orchestral accompaniment)

The Best Known Trade Mark in the world. Look to it.

List Post Free.
The Gramophone Co. Ltd., Hayes, Middlesex.

His Master's Voice

A Manchester Tenants Defence Association had been formed in 1915 with plans to distribute leaflets to 50,000 householders with the expectation that 10,000 would sign up as members of the Association to act against landlords who 'act[ed] unreasonably'.

Two months later at the general election, the Federation fielded thirty candidates across the country, contesting the Manchester Hulme seat and another at Ashton-under-Lyne. In Hulme they came fourth, taking 3.6 per cent of the total vote, but in Ashton-under-Lyne they polled 41.7 per cent of the vote. While Ashton-under-Lyne was outside the city it is interesting to observe that the Federation's election agent had commented that 'in some of the wards the pledges redeemed for the ex-soldier represented

3 to 1 in their favour. Virtually the whole of the "back streets" were solid and there was a strong soldiers' vote.[12]

The polling had been fairly heavy, which was not replicated across Manchester or Salford. Despite a day when the sun shone and there was a gentle breeze the turnout was disappointing – just 55 per cent in Manchester and even lower at 53 per cent in Salford. There was little in the way of party activity, leaving the streets empty of banners, partisan colours or election cars. Only in Hulme was there an election stir occasioned by the presence of a steam lorry hired by the Federation and decked out with huge placards, which one observer thought 'lacked the dash of the motor-car but it atoned for this defect by bulk and noise and by acting as the rallying-point to the children of Hulme.' It was, it seems, pretty much the only bit of traditional electioneering and the lacklustre tone of the day continued when the polls closed at eight o'clock with none of the usual migration into the city to wait in Albert Square for the results.

That said, large numbers of women electors went out to vote and the turnout was particularly good in Rusholme and Moss Side. In Withington it was estimated that about half the women entitled to vote had done so; in Hulme the figure was put at between 40 and 47 per cent while in Blackley it was believed to be somewhere around 80-85 per cent.

In St Michael's Ward the turnout was far better than in Cheetham Hill, where it may have been as low as 25 per cent, but in general the turnout across the city by constituency was disappointing. In Ardwick it was 47 per cent, in Blackley 50 per cent, Clayton 57 per cent, Exchange 50 per cent, Gorton 57 per cent, Hulme 52 per cent, Moss Side 50 per cent and Rusholme 62 per cent, with Withington on just 46 per cent.

Nor were the figures any better amongst the soldiers' vote. The absent voters list for Salford numbered 23,346, of which only 4,270 were returned together with 100 proxy votes. The figures for Manchester were similar.

One reason for the poor turnout for Salford may have been due to mistakes made by the military in supplying the correct address, but there does seem to have been a degree of dissatisfaction with the slowness of demobilization, with many of the Manchester ballot papers having the words 'Demobilisation first' and 'Demobilise us first' written across them.

The results altered the balance in the parliamentary seats with the Liberals losing their two MPs and the Conservatives gaining eight seats and Labour two.

NOTES

1 'The lamps are going out all over Europe; we shall not see them lit again in our life-time', Grey, Sir Edward, *Twenty-Five Years, 1892–1916*, p. 20
2 Stedman Michael, *Manchester Pals*, 1994, Leo Cooper
3 How the News came to Manchester, *Manchester Guardian*, 12 November 1918
4 Ibid., Howard Wild, 9 and 14 November 1918
5 The 8th Manchester's The City Hands Back their Colours, *Manchester Guardian*, 23 December 1918
6 Influenza Epidemic at its Height in Manchester, *Manchester Guardian*, 30 November 1918
7 Fight the Flu, advert in the *Manchester Guardian*, 15 August 1918
8 Women's Emancipation, Manchester Celebrates the Passing of the Act, *Manchester Guardian*, 11 February 1918
9 Christmas Comforts Funds for the men who have to stand by, *Manchester Guardian*, 11 November 1918
10 Dr Marion Phillips, The Soldier's Pay, *Manchester Guardian*, 9 November 1914
11 L.C. Evans, Secretary to the Salford War Pensions Committee, letter to the *Manchester Guardian*, 14 June 1918
12 Ashton-under-Lyne, the Soldier's Candidate, *Manchester Guardian*, 16 December 1918

6

LEGACY

The Great War has joined that long list of conflicts that are now confined to history. Those who served in our armed forces, toiled in the munitions factories and tendered the sick and wounded are all gone. So too are many of the children who were growing up during those four years. And with their passing many of the personal links to the conflict have been severed.

Tom Fox of the Manchester Regiment.

Of course the war is well documented in books, documents and photographs that sit beside the official records. But for many of us the most enduring reminder of the conflict will be the monuments honouring those who took part. They include the Cenotaph outside the Town Hall, the smaller crosses, and the Rolls of Honour erected in churches and outside public and commercial buildings. To these can be added the personal tributes commissioned by grieving families which range from an inscription on a gravestone to beautifully crafted scrolls that once took pride of place in the family home.

Of all these it will be the Cenotaph that many will identify with. It was unveiled on 12 July 1924 and the ceremony was led by Mrs Bingle from Rylance Street in Ancoats, along with Lord Derby. Mrs Bingle had lost her three sons and it seemed fitting that she should be at the centre of the city's act of remembrance. While Lord Derby had been closely associated with recruiting men for the war and will forever be linked with the Pals battalions, it was Mrs Bingle who was the more significant choice.

The family were originally from Stroud in Gloucestershire but had settled in the eastern side of the city by 1899, and in the years before the Great War did not appear to stray far from Rylance Street in Ardwick. It was an area of densely packed terraced housing, dominated by the railway depot to the south and surrounded by iron and steel works, along with the Bradford Colliery and countless smaller enterprises. Here they brought up eight children in houses ranging in size from three rooms to five. Mr Bingle was engaged in making umbrellas, their eldest son was a career soldier, another was a postman and their youngest son an errand boy.

History has been capricious with the details of the boys' military careers and all we know of the eldest son, Ernest Albert, was that he had enlisted by the time he was 18 in 1901 and at his death had reached the rank of sergeant. His brother, Charles Henry, was a gunner and Nelson Allen, the youngest of the three, was a 2nd Corporal in the Royal Engineers. Some of Nelson Allen's army records have survived which show that he signed up at Ardwick in April 1915, aged 19.

A replica of Manchester Cenotaph belonging to the family of Private Joseph Thomas.

It is so little for what amounted to such a great sacrifice and the enormity of that loss must have been overwhelming, more so because all three died in the final year of the war. Nelson Allen, aged 21, was killed in the March, Ernest Albert on 8 May and Charles Henry on the 27th.

Before the unveiling ceremony the Lord Mayor had spoken of how all sides in the conflict had suffered, adding that there were just as many broken hearts in the conquering country as there were in the conquered. The ceremony closed with a procession of women carrying flowers, which were spread at the foot of the monument.[1]

Similar scenes were repeated across Manchester during the early 1920s as communities along with businesses and the Corporation unveiled memorials. The Manchester and Lancashire Family History Society has recorded a total of 153 in its ongoing project to list them all. Many echo the simplicity of the Cenotaph, incorporating a cross and a set of panels recording those who served. Others, like the memorials at Victoria Station and the Print Works, consist of a large brass plaque. Nor are all of them to be found in the large public places like churches, schools and workplaces. A significant number were created by social clubs and it is these which are perhaps most at risk because when a club closes its plaque may be lost, scrapped, or end up in private hands. When the Chorlton Conservative Club closed in 2012 its memorial was saved and is now on display in Southern Cemetery. Others, like that of the Stretford Conservative Association, made its way through a dealer into a collection.

Less at risk but often hidden away in an archive are the records produced by various companies recording their staff who fought. Listed in the Lancashire and Yorkshire Banks' Roll of Honour is Cyril Hopewood Bowman, who worked at the Portland Street branch. He was 29 years old when he enlisted in the 2nd City Battalion on 3 September 1914, and was posted to France in November the following year. Apart from a short break in 1917, when he came home and married Mabel Frost, he remained on the Western Front, where he was wounded and finally demobbed in March 1919. On his return to civilian life he

Roll of Honour,
Manchester
Corporation.

ROLL OF HONOUR
OF THE
Manchester Corporation
List of Employees who have joined the Colours.

City Architect's Department.

ANDREW, F. W.	GAUL, M.	PEARSON, R.
ARNOLD, E. D.	JAMES, H.	GRIMSHAW, C. E.
GAUL, E. P.	MITCHELL, W. H.	

City Art Gallery.

CORNTHWAITE, W. E.- 1/2nd East Lancs. R.F.A.
RICHARDS, W. - - - - 17th S.Bt. Manchester Rgt.
HALLEY, J. C. - - - 3/8th Bt. Lanc. Fus. (T.F.).

Heaton Park Branch Gallery.

POWELL, F. - - - - - Army Reservist, R.A.M.C.

Queen's Park Branch Gallery.

TAIT, F. W. - - - - - 9th Bt. Royal Scots H.
BOWDEN, J. - - - - - 18th S.Bt. Manchester Rgt.

Baths Department.

BEAVER, A. E.	HUMPHREYS, G.	MUSGROVE, S.
BEIRNE, P.	JACOB, A. E.	PATE, L. A.
BISHOP, A.	KAY, W.	PENDER, A.
BLAGBROUGH, W. J.	LOWTH, C.	PRINCE, C. H.
BROWN, J.	MAHER, A.	PRINCE, T.
CARTER, J.	MAHER, T.	PUGH, J.
CHARLESWORTH, S.	MCKEIVER, L.	ROWORTH, L.
CORDT, J. P.	MARLAND, J	ROYLE, H.
CORDT, T. H.	MAYCOCK, C.	SMITH, J. W.
COTTON, G.	MORRISSEY, D.	SMITH, G.
CURRELL, N.	(Died in hospital, the	STEARNE, T.
DAVIES, T. H.	result of wounds).	WILLIAMS, R. H.
DICKENSON, H.	MOWATT, S. B.	WRENSHALL, F.
FRANCIS, W.		

404 a

settled down with Mabel in Attwood Road in Didsbury, where
he remained until his death in 1954.

Fortunately, his service records have survived and we know
that he was 5ft 7in tall, weighed 114lbs, had brown eyes, black
hair, with a ruddy complexion and that after he had been
wounded his mother wrote requesting that he be transferred to
clerical work. He also appears in The Manchester City Battalions
Book of Honour, published by Sherratt & Hughes in 1916. It is,
in the words of Lord Derby who wrote the Foreword, 'a fitting
record of the magnificent patriotism which has inspired that
area since the beginning of the War.'[2] Here are included not just

the names of the men who enlisted but their unit and battalion, along with photographs of each company and the individual Rolls of Honour of 306 Manchester businesses. It is a powerful resource in its own right as well as a moving record and it too has been transcribed by the Manchester and Lancashire Family History Society and made available online by Findmypast.

The individual Rolls of Honour range from that of Hall & Pickles of 64 Port Street, which lists sixteen names, to Manchester Corporation whose roll runs to thirty pages, covering every department from Baths to Cleansing, Markets and the police, to tram workers and teachers.

Many Rolls of Honour would also be the subject of special memorial services like the one at St Mark's in West Gorton, held on 2 February 1923 for the dedication of the 'War Memorial Reredos and Panels'. The Right Revd Bishop Taylor Smith led the service, which consisted of a series of hymns and readings culminating with an address and finally the blessing. The bishop then dedicated the memorial 'To the Glory of God and in grateful memory of those who gave their lives for King and Country and a righteous cause … May all that look upon it realize the peace of sins forgiven, the joy of faithful service, and the power of an endless life to which may God Vouchsafe to bring us all, through Jesus Christ our Lord.' After the haunting Last Post and the Bishop's Address, the service concluded with the rousing 'Mine eyes have seen the glory of the coming of the Lord'.

In all 192 names were included on the panels, of which one was Private Alan Barber of the Royal Fusiliers. He had been a salesman before the war,

Roll of Honour, Wesleyan church, Gorton.

" Heroes All "
Belonging to
Wesleyan Church
and
Sunday School,
Cross Lane, Gorton,
Manchester.

" Lest we Forget."

Private John Edmund Shepherd of the Manchester's died at Gallipoli on 30 May 1915.

John Edmund Shepherd
Age 19
1ST 7TH Batt: Man/r   Regiment (T)
Duty Called, Duty Done, He Died a Noble Death.

living with his parents and two siblings in Gorton. He died on 17 October 1918 aged 23 and is buried at the Highland Cemetery at Le Cateau in northern France. He was the eldest of Mr and Mrs Barber's three children.

Perhaps the most telling are the personal memorials created by grieving families. Most take the form of a simple inscription on a gravestone but others are more elaborate. Of these some are lavishly handcrafted in stone and meant for a church or chapel, but others are more modest and designed to be displayed in the home.

The one for young John Edmund Shepherd, who died on 30 May 1915 aged 19 during the Gallipoli Campaign, is made of paper on card and measures 37.5cm by 24.5cm. It carries the flags of the six Allied nations either side of an oval insert which contains his picture and has the simple inscription, 'Duty Called, Duty Done, He Died a Noble Death'.

Among the Commonwealth war graves in Southern Cemetery are those of Australian, New Zealand and Canadian soldiers. Of the twenty-six men of the Canadian Expeditionary Force is the grave of Thomas John of the Machine Gun Corps, who died on 6 November 1918.

It has survived the century although is now a little battered at one edge and shows evidence that it was once in a frame, and no doubt moved with the family from Moss Side to Heaton Mersey and eventually to Withington. His parents died in the early 1930s when his memorial scroll passed to his brother Harold, who had also served with the Red Cross during the war. For many years now it has formed part of a permanent exhibition of memorabilia from the Great War which is part of a much larger collection of material from both world wars belonging to David Harrop.

It is fitting that his exhibition should be in Southern Cemetery because this is where Private Shepherd's parents and his youngest brother are buried. Some of the medals, letters and photographs in that exhibition are also connected with men who are either buried in the cemetery or are honoured there. They include the grave of James Arthur Parkes, who died in 1917 aged 64, and who is sometimes credited as the oldest soldier from Manchester to die during the Great War. His military career stretched back to the nineteenth century, but he died in Chorlton and not on a battlefield. That said, his headstone records that two of his sons died serving abroad.

Sergeant David Parkes of the 21st Battalion of the Manchester Regiment was killed on 12 January 1917, while his brother Alfred of the 2nd Battalion of the Manchester's died in a prisoner-of-war camp on 27 May 1918. Neither is buried in the family plot: David is in the war cemetery at Arras and Alfred in Cologne. But both appear on the headstone and the memorial includes a carved sword and military cap. Their father had re-enlisted in August 1915 and worked at the recruitment centres at Houldsworth Hall, Deansgate and at the Town Hall.

*Postcard from the
20th City Battalion,
January 1917.*

In all there are 803 remembered in the cemetery either on individual headstones or on the large screen which is maintained by the Commonwealth War Graves Commission.

A century after the war began some of those who served and died are being honoured afresh. Many of the memorials have been cleaned or restored and some even moved to a more suitable place. They include the gateway at Victoria Station through which thousands of soldiers departed the city for the battlefields and through which also arrived many of the wounded. For years the arch stood slightly neglected, first with a set of closed doors and later a small unremarkable wooden gate. On busy commuter days I doubt that many people gave much time to the plaque commemorating the 'MEMORY OF THE MANY THOUSANDS OF MEN WHO PASSED THROUGH THIS DOOR TO THE GREAT WAR 1914-1919 AND OF THOSE WHO DID NOT RETURN', but during the recent modernization of the railway station a huge glass panel has been inserted into the arch recording the places the British Army saw action and listing the casualties. It is a simple and yet imaginative way of restoring the significance of the gateway.

Manchester City Council chose to name a road in Chorlton after William Eric Lunt, who was born on Sandy Lane. He had enlisted on 5 September 1915, was wounded and died two days later of his wounds. It is a small but touching memorial to a young man whose name had faded into the shadows.

More recently a memorial to the men of the London Road Goods Depot was unveiled at Piccadilly Railway Station. The original had been dedicated 'TO THE MEMORY OF OUR COMRADES WHO SACRIFICED THEIR LIVES IN THE SERVICE OF THEIR COUNTRY DURING THE EUROPEAN WAR AND AS A TRIBUTE TO THE 580 MEN WHO SERVED'.

It stood on London Road but was lost during the alterations to the railway station in the early 1960s. However, through the research of Mr Wayne McDonald and Mr Andy Partington and with the support of Virgin Trains and the Railway Heritage Trust, a new memorial has been made and now stands on platform 10/11 at Piccadilly Railway Station.[3] Amongst those present at the unveiling were family members of some of the men who appear on the memorial, and two women who discovered that they shared a relative on the monument.

For many the passing of a century has done nothing to break the link with those who served. For some it will have led them to trace their family member through the official records, perhaps even visiting the battlefields and writing their individual stories. For others it will be in discovering a long forgotten photograph, a collection of letters or even an item of uniform. And of these very physical legacies it will be medals which are the most tangible connection with the past.

Aside from those awarded for bravery, four service medals were issued after the war. These were the 1914 Star for men who had served in France or Belgium from 5 August 1914 through to 22 November of the same year, the 1914-15 Star for those who served abroad from August 1914 to December 1915, and the British War Medal and Allied Victory Medal.

All medals have their own story, like that of Private William Edwards who received the British War Medal. He joined the 1st City Battalion at the outbreak of the war, was wounded at Gallipoli in 1915 and died at home in Moss Side on 22 November 1918, just ten days after the Armistice, and was buried in Southern Cemetery.

George Davison, who died in June 1918, received the British War Medal, Allied Victory Medal and the large bronze Memorial Plaque, issued to the wives and next of kin of all those killed in the war. Of the three it is the bronze Memorial Plaque which is the most impressive. It measures 122mm in diameter and depicts an image of Britannia holding a trident and standing beside a lion. Two dolphins swim around Britannia and a second lion appears at the bottom. Each plaque carried the name of the dead serviceman, omitting any reference to rank, and with the inscription 'He died for Freedom and Honour' – which was changed to 'She died for Freedom and Honour' for the 600 issued to commemorate women. In all 1,355,000 were made and they continued to be produced into the 1930s in recognition of those who died of their wounds after the war.

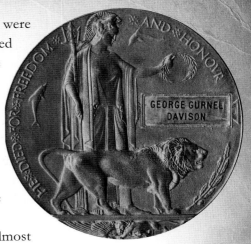

The first were made in Acton in London and later production was transferred to the Royal Arsenal in Woolwich, which was just a short distance from where George Davison had been stationed in 1915. Each plaque also came with a scroll.

Bronze plaque of George Davison.

In some cases a family will have an almost intact set of medals and other personal effects, but even when that amounts to just one document it is enough to start a search which tells a story. And for the Fisher family that story turned on one Red Cross postcard sent to Mrs Emily Fisher in April 1916. She had written to the Red Cross asking for help to track her husband Private James Fisher, who had gone missing in July of the previous year. He was in the 2nd Battalion of the Lancashire Fusiliers. They suggested she contacted the records office at Preston and also a fellow soldier in the '11th platoon of the 2nd Lancs [who] may be able to tell you something about your husband. Meanwhile we are continuing our enquiries.'

The news when it came was not good. Private Fisher had died on 7 July 1915. According to one report he and five other soldiers had taken shelter in a cottage when the shelling started but the cottage suffered a direct hit and they were all killed. His name is recorded on the Menin Gate Memorial at Ypres.

The couple had been married for just eight years and Emily was left to bring up their adopted son. Private Fisher was 29 years of age when he was killed, and Emily a year younger. After the war Mrs Fisher remarried and continued to live in the family home until 1967, when she moved in with her son. She died in 1973.

But what followed was one of those remarkable twists which led from that Red Cross postcard to a conversation with Mrs

'Private J. Fisher missing in action': the Red Cross postcard sent to Mrs Fisher in April 1916.

New Telephone No.—REGENT 6151.

Enquiry Department for Wounded and Missing:

18, CARLTON HOUSE TERRACE, S.W.

Apr: 5. 1916

✚ BRITISH RED CROSS
AND
ORDER OF ST. JOHN

Pte J. Fisher, 9028, D. Co. 2nd Lancs. Fus.
We have received a suggestion that if you wrote to Pte. Hinchcliffe, C. Co., 2nd Lancs. Fus. c/o Record Office, Preston, marked "to be forwarded:- + also to Pte Farrington C. Co., 11th platoon, 2nd Lancs. Fus., B. E. F., they may be able to tell you something about your husband. Meanwhile we are continuing our enquiries as before (for Sir L. Mallet) yours truly p E. re- Matcham

Mrs Fisher, on the left, date unknown.

Fisher's grandson that took me to the collection which has made this book possible.

Their grandson, Ken Fisher, came across both the postcard and the medals in an exhibition in the Central Reference Library and while reading the notes he realised that one of the medals belonged to his grandfather, James Fisher. The staff put him in touch with David Harrop, who had another medal belonging to his granddad's brother, whom he knew nothing about.

That chance visit just goes to show that by carefully studying the letters, pictures and official records, many of which are now online, it is possible to rediscover something of the lives of those who otherwise are just names on a memorial.

Meanwhile, for those who could command better wages, their standard of life improved. The anecdotal evidence from Robert Roberts, that keen observer of all that went on, suggests that in his bit of Salford abject poverty was beginning to disappear by 1916. Children looked better fed, there was money for 'luxuries', nights out, and a growing trend among some of his mother's customers to ask for the less basic food stuffs.

There is no doubt that for many women the war offered up new horizons, even if these were mitigated by unequal pay and the prejudice of some of their male colleagues. Some at least got the vote, some were earning far more than they might have done before the war, and many had a new self-confidence in themselves and what they could achieve. Some of these changes were already in play, which the war merely sped up. Women were being employed in greater numbers across industry and commerce through to the professions long before 1914.

Of course how these changes impacted on an individual depends on what we know about them and sadly in most cases is never enough. With the passage of a century many of the documents are lost, some remain out of bounds and most letters, photographs and other possessions have gone. If we are lucky there will be stories passed down to us but these will be selective and will fade with time.

George and Nellie Davison

Born in 1886 in Harpurhey, George Davison began his married life in Hulme in 1908, served in the Royal Artillery and had been in the Burnley Volunteer Training Corps for part of 1914, coming away with a medal and appearing in two pictures taken of the Volunteers on parade in front of St John the Evangelist Church in the village of Worsthorne on the edge of Burnley.

The following year he was in Woolwich in London and writing home to his wife that he was not overly impressed with his new quarters. He reported that there were no beds, limited blankets and little to do outside the training routines.

At the same time, like most men far away from home and family, he fretted over what was going on in Manchester. On more than one occasion his concern was for the health of both his wife, Nellie, and son, Duncan, as seen in this letter from November 1915:

> I am very sorry to hear that Duncan has been seriously ill. I would not like to lose him for the world itself. If anything serious occurs again to either of you, get a Doctor's note (they can be got for the asking if you tell him I am on active service and you want to see me) and send it at once. Remember it will take at least 1½ days to reach me (unless you send a Telegram) and it takes two days for me to get home so that there must be no time wasted.

George Davison was killed in action in June 1918 and his widow was faced with a succession of official documents which stretched on into the early 1920s.

It started with his last will, which he had made in March 1918 in Woolwich shortly before embarking for the Western Front. It was witnessed by H.M. Drinkhall and V.L. Dade, and was handwritten on a single sheet of note-paper and is simple and to the point: 'This is the last will and testament of me George Gurnel Davison of Birch Vale Cottage, Romiley, Cheshire. I give, devise and bequeath to my dear wife Mary Ellen all my property whatsoever and wheresoever and I appoint her sole Executor of this my will.'

Nellie Davison and her son
Duncan, c. 1915.

His wife also kept the letters from the War Department announcing his death, a letter from an officer describing the manner of death, and much correspondence about pensions. Amongst these were a series of press cuttings, each just a few lines, ranging from 'Davison. - In loving remembrance of Bombardier GEORGE G. DAVISON, killed in action June 17, 1918. WIFE and SON', to 'DAVISON.-L/Bombardier G.G. DAVISON. QQ5100, Royal Field Artillery, killed in action June 17, 1918. Ever remembered by his WIFE and little Son.'

In all there are six cuttings carefully preserved along with his letters, medals and pictures.

So it is with Mrs Nellie Davison, who lost her husband in June 1918 and never remarried. After she left Hulme she returned to Romiley and that is where the trail ends. The last item in the collection is dated 1954 and that is a single piece of correspondence relating to a week's touring holiday of southern England. How she lived her life after the Great War is unknown, although records suggest she died in 1965 and her son, Duncan, in 1999.

The will of George Davison, made in Woolwich before leaving for France.

There is one twist in the story. The war letters refer to a Mr and Mrs Drinkal who lived in Eltham in south east London. Nellie in all probability stayed with Mrs Drinkal in 1915 and her husband may also have been billeted in the same house. It formed part of an estate built during the war for the families of munitions workers employed at the Royal Arsenal in Woolwich. I grew up in one of those houses and Mr and Mrs Drinkal lived in another just across the road.

It was my friend Tricia Leslie who tracked down the house after I told her of the possible connection and while it wouldn't warrant even the smallest footnote in a history of the Great War it has significance for me. Having spent three years with the George Davison collection I never expected that our families would end up living next door to each other.

NOTES

1 The *Manchester Guardian*, 14 July 1924
2 Lord Derby, Foreword, *The Manchester City Battalions Book of Honour, 1916*, Sherratt & Hughes
3 The memorial was unveiled on 4 May 2016

7

POSTSCRIPT

Souvenir from the Great War.

Like many of my generation the Great War did not loom as large as the war that followed it. The evidence for that later conflict was still all around us, from bombsites and those classic British war films of the 1950s to the stories that filled the comics we read. By contrast the Great War was more distant and rarely talked about. Added to which those who had lived through it, like my grandfather, his brother and my uncles, had long ago put that bit of their youth behind them.

It would be years later, as I began picking my way through our family history, that their contribution became clear. We can count a great-grandfather, a grandfather, two great-uncles and two uncles who joined the Colours, and because my maternal grandmother was German there will be her brothers and cousins who served in the forces of Imperial Germany.

But apart from a few letters, two photographs and parts of their service records, that time in their lives is a blank. Ironically the most complete set of military records are those for one of my great-uncles who served with the Canadian Expeditionary Force. His details were kept in Canada while those of the rest of the family, along with a large number of other service records, were destroyed during an air raid in the Second World War.

Embroidered silk postcard of the Lancashire Fusiliers.

This is a real personal loss, but the passage of a century would never have been kind to that sort of material. So much that was official, from ration books to identity cards, would have been thrown out without a second thought in the years after the war, while letters were lost and pictures got handed around till they were too battered and creased to be of much use.

All of which means that this book would never have been possible were it not for a fine collection of memorabilia held by David Harrop. It is quite unique in that it includes everything from letters, photographs and medals to those items which seldom survive, and a large part of it is directly related to Manchester. David allowed me to roam at will through the collection, made helpful suggestions, and was not above sourcing fresh material for the book. His contribution is much appreciated and has made it possible to bring out of the shadows many of those who lived through the Great War in the city. And, on a personal note, it has brought me a little closer to the members of my own family who were involved in the war. They never talked about their experiences and I never asked.

The opportunity to read the letters, newspaper stories and official records as well as handling many of the everyday objects they would have known has made the link with this part of their lives and that, after all, is what history should be about.

George Bradford Simpson (1899–2000), c. 1918.

Message from the Queen to George Bradford Simpson on his 100th birthday in 1999.

Windsor Castle by Paul Hogarth

ABOUT THE AUTHOR

ANDREW SIMPSON writes and lectures on the history of Chorlton-cum-Hardy and Manchester. He retired from teaching after thirty-five years and has been active in the politics of the city for over forty years. He is the author of *The Story of Chorlton-cum-Hardy*, has collaborated on *Didsbury Through Time*, *The Story of Hough End Hall* and *Manchester Pubs*, and is currently writing a book on the history of the Manchester and Salford Boys' and Girls' Refuges and Homes as well as also working on a history of Alexandra Park. Andrew lives in Chorlton.

BIBLIOGRAPHY

BOOKS

Bowser, Thekla, *Britain's Civilian Volunteers; Authorised Story of British Voluntary Aid Detachment Work in the Great War*, 1917, Moffat, Yard & Co.

Graham, John W., *Conscription and Conscience: A History, 1916-1919*, 1922, George Allen & Unwin Ltd

Grey, Sir Edward, *Twenty-five Years, 1892–1916* [n.p.]

Hartley, John, *6th Battalion of the Manchester Regiment in the Great War*, 2010, Pen & Sword

HMSO, *Official History of the Ministry of Munitions, Volume 1: Industrial Mobilisation, 1914-1915*, 2009, Imperial War Museum

Liddlington, Jill, *The Long Road to Greenham*, 1989, Virago Press Ltd

O'Neill, Joseph, *Manchester in the Great War*, 2014, Pen and Sword

Rea, Anthony, *Manchester's Little Italy*, 1988, Neil Richardson

Roberts, Robert, *A Ragged Schooling*, 1976, Manchester University Press

Roberts, Robert, *The Classic Slum: Salford Life in the First Quarter of the Century*, 1971, Pelican edition, 1973

Stedman Michael, *Manchester Pals*, 1994, Leo Cooper

Storey, Neil R. and Housego, Molly, *Women in the First World War*, 2010, Shire Publications

The Manchester Battalions Book of Honour, 1916, Sherratt & Hughes

NEWSPAPERS & MAGAZINES

Daily Citizen, 20 March 1915

Daily Mirror, 7 June 1916

Manchester Guardian, 1914–1919

St Clements Parish Church Magazine, October 1917

ARTICLES

'A History of Manchester Suburbs: Chorlton', *Manchester Evening News*, 20 September 1901

Pearce, Cyril, Typical Conscientious Objectors – A Better Class of Conscience? No-Conscription Fellowship Image Management and the Manchester Contribution, Manchester Regional History Review, 2004

2nd Western General Hospital, Manchester, 1914–1919, Manchester, 1919, Charles Server

OTHER SOURCES

Archives of the Together Trust

Davison Collection, letters, personal papers and official documents, 1899–1959

Housing Conditions in Manchester & Salford, A Report Prepared for the Citizens' Association for the Improvement of the Unwholesome Dwellings and Surroundings of People, T.R. Marr, Sherratt and Hughes, 1904

Manchester City Battalions Book of Honour, 1916, Sherratt & Hughes

National Registration Act 1915

Red Cross Hospital, East Lancashire Branch of the British Red Cross Society, Sherratt & Hughes, 1916

Slater's Manchester, Salford & Suburban Directory, 1911

The Great War and the North West, Nick Mansfield (ed.), 2013, Manchester Region History Review, Vol. 24

The London Food Vigilance Committee, 1915, Archives & Study Centre, The People's History Museum

The War Emergency Workers National Committee, Collected Papers, Archives & Study Centre, The People's History Museum

Wild, Harold, The Diary of a Conscientious Objector, 1915–1919, Dorothy Spence (ed.)

Wild, Harold, letter to Dorothy Spence (*nèe* Wild), 17 November 1974

Women's War Interests, Work of the Manchester and District Committee, The Common Cause, 3 March 1916, Archives & Study Centre, The People's History Museum

INDEX

Great War Britain: The First World War at Home

Luci Gosling

After the declaration of war in 1914, the conflict dominated civilian life for the next four years. Magazines quickly adapted without losing their gossipy essence: fashion jostled for position with items on patriotic fundraising, and court presentations were replaced by notes on nursing. The result is a fascinating, amusing and uniquely feminine perspective of life on the home front.
978 0 7524 9188 2

The Workers' War: British Industry and the First World War

Anthony Burton

The First World War didn't just rock the nation in terms of bloodshed: it was a war of technological and industrial advances. Working Britain experienced change as well: with the men at war, it fell to the women of the country to keep the factories going. Anthony Burton explores that change.
978 0 7524 9886 7

Visit our website and discover many other First World War books.

www.thehistorypress.co.uk/first-world-war